Hell and the Gospel

Kurios Christos

That every tongue would confess that Jesus Christ is Lord -
Phil 2:11

Hell and the Gospel

Examining the Doctrine of Hell as It Relates to the Wisdom, Holiness, Justice, and Mercy of the Lord

JASON TACKETT

RESOURCE *Publications* • Eugene, Oregon

HELL AND THE GOSPEL
Examining the Doctrine of Hell as It Relates to the Wisdom, Holiness, Justice, and Mercy of the Lord

Resource Publications
An Imprint of Wipf and Stock Publishers
199 W. 8th Ave., Suite 3
Eugene, OR 97401

www.wipfandstock.com

PAPERBACK ISBN: 979-8-3852-4596-3
HARDCOVER ISBN: 979-8-3852-4597-0
EBOOK ISBN: 979-8-3852-4598-7

05/02/25

All Scripture references use the King James Version of the Bible.

Contents

Introduction

IT IS THE SINGULAR intent of this humble work to declare the necessity of the doctrine of Hell as it is declared by the Scriptures. Seeing that it is impossible for any of us to start from ourselves and declare what will be after death, we must declare ourselves from the beginning to be completely dependent upon revelation for what we believe will be our end. If God has not spoken, then all discussion of what will be is vain. If He has, we cannot go beyond what He has said. As long as we stand at our own vantage point, we know nothing of that undiscovered country and know little to nothing of how our present is connected to that which will be. We stand in ignorance; totally dependent on a voice from outside to speak of its truth.

Eschatology, along with all other theological or philosophical inquiry, cannot start with our autonomous thoughts or experience and draw anything other than unfounded speculation. We have no empirical access to what will be from our experience. The test tube or the scientific method cannot discover the result of our final judgment, and we have no philosophical deductions that can ground us firmly in the substance of that coming day. But there is a God that has spoken who knows the end from the beginning and has allowed us to peer past the current moment through the veil of our ignorance to see what is indeed after this.

Being dependent upon what God has said, the discussion that will follow will speak of Hell as a concept that is declared by the God of truth. It is not something we know by rational or empirical means and therefore, cannot be defeated or denied on those grounds. The main tension inevitably lies here; in between the revelation of Hell by God and the rebellious and autonomous declaration by man (the pseudo-rational and pseudo-empirical man) for there is no rational or empirical knowledge that there is no Hell without the revelation of God.

Ultimately, there are only two views of Hell presented in this work. There is Hell as it is declared by God, and there is Hell as it is denied to some degree or another by the reasoning of man. And the goal of this work is to side with what God has revealed and to reject what He has not revealed. Other greater works on this subject may focus on comparing and contrasting various views and their subtle shades of meaning, but this author cannot be persuaded that anything else is pertinent to the subject of Hell other than the question, "Do you believe what God has said?"

There are various views that uphold Hell as a concept that will not be the direct thrust of the following discussion though they will be mentioned. Keep in mind though that it is not our present purpose to conceptualize Hell outside of the Scriptures. There are generally three views that affirm Hell. There is the *restorative view* that sees Hell as a fearful, conceptual step toward ultimate salvation. That is, they see Hell as merging ultimately with the Catholic idea of purgatory. It is a place where the wicked go in order to be purged from their sin or impurity. Hell is, in this sense, a step toward heaven. It upholds the false idea of the ultimate universal salvation of all. While there will be no direct attempt to refute this idea, it suffers from the inability to maintain faithfulness to the text. And those would be the greatest marks against it. There is no indication in the text that universal salvation will be a reality. It is better to submit to the text since we cannot reason autonomously in this matter. We desire nothing of a speculative theology.

Another affirmation of Hell sees it as a steppingstone toward annihilation. This view is called conditionalism, or the *conditional view*, and it is far closer to a scriptural affirmation than restorationism. It says that Hell is the fearful reality that one must face as a mechanism toward their eventual extinction. It too suffers from, in the mind of this writer, difficulties with the natural understanding of the words that God moved His prophets to speak. If the goal is fidelity to God, then this view must answer to the plain understanding of the text.

The final affirmation of Hell is the *traditional view*. It is this view that is presented in this work that will be stood in opposition to the view that there is no Hell. Note that the other two views see Hell as a step toward something else. The Scriptural view however, is that Hell is the final state of the lost. The traditional view is the natural understanding of what the text of the Scriptures say about the subject. The affirmations of Hell (from restorationism, to conditionalism, to traditionalism) rise and fall with their dependence upon what the text actually says. There is some room for differences in these perspectives, but there is no room for setting aside the text to believe some autonomous line of reasoning. All of these views affirm that Hell is real and Hell is fearful, but they are not all equally submitted to believing what God has said.

The contention of this treatise is honoring what God has said. Those who wish to deny the reality of Hell by reducing it to metaphor or deny its finality on the basis of their own reasoning do so in error. To deny the existence of Hell is not simply to dismiss as meaningless the uncomfortable idea of suffering yet to be. If one denies Hell they are throwing out the idea of judgment and morality, concepts that draw directly from revelational truth. Without the voice from outside humanity all is reduced to the here and the now. There is no justice without final judgment. By destroying Hell one destroys the hope of heaven, as well. Further, they destroy the idea that what we do here has meaning and has value in any ultimate sense. They destroy the patience of the saints that suffer under the hands of the wicked in this life; those who rob and steal with impunity and die fat and full on the plunder of their covetousness. Hell is not something that can simply be dismissed without reverberating effects on meaning and morality.

More than anything, one cannot dismiss the concept of Hell and maintain a meaningful doctrine of Lordship. The God of the Scriptures is one that is able to destroy both body and soul in Hell (Matt 10:28). The denial of Hell says that no such God exists. It makes man their own god, and history has shown already what a pitiful god man is. The Christian does not believe in or declare any philosophy of ethics that ignores the absolute Lordship of God over all that we do or think. We may call this *Lordship ethics*. It is not *normative ethics* that defines our reality as if society alone has defined what we should and should not do and as if our judgment goes no further than our social context. It is not *personal ethics* that rules over man as if man had no one to answer to except himself. Moral reality is not wrapped up in man's own thoughts and opinions of his own actions. Nor is the ethical reality of man simply *deontological* in nature as if there are some abstract impersonal principles out there somewhere that judge our actions indifferently. Ethical reality begins with Christ as Lord (recognizing that truth) and living in relationship with what He has declared to be. We must call Him Lord and be obedient to Him, and to fail to live in that ethical light is to be worthy of judgment (John 8:24). We will stand before the Lord that has commanded, who is holy and righteous, and to whom we must give an account.

Hell is the fearful doctrine that judgment or accounting will occur. Like Pharaoh, the rebel may say now, "Who is the Lord that I should obey Him?" But at that future time, they must answer for that rebellious ethic. No one in this world may claim autonomy from their Lord in safety. Hell is the truth that disobedience to the Lord cannot ultimately be allowed to continue in this moral universe. "Fear him which is able to destroy both soul and body in hell" (Matt 10:28).

The affirmation or denial of Hell boils down to one's right relationship with God as Lord of all. Are you prepared to face the implications that a denial of Hell implies? I know it is uncomfortable to consider the reality of Hell, but is it not equally troubling to negate its reality? What is the alternative to a belief in Hell? You can in its denial believe in a world without morality (without final judgment there is no ultimate value to any choice we make). You can believe in a world where the wicked triumph (for this life alone would show the final score). You can believe in a world without meaning (without final judgment whereby works are evaluated, no act has any ultimate meaning). You can do all those knowing that you have refused to hear what the Lord has spoken.

I would like to offer something better to you, the affirmation that God is true with all the hope and assurance that comes from such an affirmation. Yes, it is a fearful reality that broached the subject of Hell, but that alone can connect us to truth and meaning. In this work I offer you the following thesis statement that sums up what I believe is what God has revealed to be true about what will be. I pray that this will be a blessing to the reader.

Thesis—*The all-wise, all-good, and just Lord of all has revealed the fearful truth and severity of His justice to be given to sinful men at the end of the age, but in His love toward the sinner has provided salvation through His Son that the sinner might flee from that wrath to come.*

PART 1

The Severity of God

"Behold therefore the goodness and severity of God: on them which fell, severity; but toward thee, goodness. . . ."

ROMANS 11:22

THE GOODNESS OF GOD, though significantly misunderstood, is an easy and even preferable topic to speak of openly. No matter the religious context, if one states that the Lord is good it will be generally readily consented to and answered with happy clichés. But if we say that God ought to be feared, for His judgment is severe and righteous, these clichés too often turn into stern resistance. If we say, "God is fearful" or "God's judgment is severe," we do not expect the jovial and welcome reply, "Amen" or "All the time!" The reason for this is that the judgment of God and His righteous wrath against sin make us uncomfortable; whereas His gracious acts of kindness do not. To face this truth is to face our own guilt and liability before God and hence, it is rightly uncomfortable.

We are so easy on ourselves for our sins, and we expect that God is just like us. The Psalmist warned us against such foolish reasoning (Ps 50:21). The assumption is that our sin is not that bad. But that is due to us not knowing the depth of our sin and its exceeding sinfulness, or what Solomon called "the plague of our own hearts." (Rom 7:11–13, I Kings 8:38) In other words, we do not know our true state in God's righteous eyes. We cannot fathom a God who would pour out His wrath without any mixture of mercy (Rev 14:10, 11), and we are convinced that we are not guilty enough to deserve such an end. When the Scriptures present us with such a truth about God we bristle against it. "That cannot be what that means," we say. However, the God of the Scriptures is contrasted as the one who shows mercy but will not clear the guilty (Ex 34:7). How far we are willing to go in our resistance to such declarations will be indicative of our faithfulness to the faith once delivered to the saints (Jude 1:3).

In the context of the judgment of God upon Israel and extension of merciful provision of Gospel benefits to the Gentile nations, Paul highlighted the need for his readers to recognize and glory both in God's goodness and His severity in judgment. On the one hand, we glory in the kindness our God gave in showing mercy to undeserving sinners. On the other hand, we are to glory in the harshness (*apotomia*) of His justice. Why? Because we recognize how good His mercy is to the undeserving by measuring it or contrasting it to what His justice actually demands. He gives grace to some who are deserving of His wrath but gives to others, after much long suffering, what they absolutely deserve. Such a God that may have mercy if He wills or may judge if He wills is the true object of our faith (Rom 9:14, 15). And in the context of the final wrath of such a God, Christ has told us that we ought to fear Him who can destroy our bodies and souls in hell (Matt 10:28). Those who refuse to worship this God have set up a false idol and have added to their guilt before Him.

Approaching the subject of Hell, a word which will mean in this treatise the final judgment of the wicked, we are asked to behold the ultimate expression of the severity or harshness of a Holy and Righteous Judge. The wicked will one day reach the end of their undeserved mercies and approach the precipice of His wrath. The sheer and sharp drop off into the fathomless reality of God's wrath against sin is the epitome of deserved severity. Words like contempt, punishment, fire, shame, eternal, everlasting, torment, weeping, and so on will be words that the writers of Scripture employ to trace out their doctrine. It is the black velvet background on which the jewel of God's mercy to undeserving sinners glitters. The goodness of which we love to speak is the kindness that will be shown by God to His saints through His Son in ages to come (Eph 2:7). That is the ultimate expression of God's goodness, and it belongs only to those saved by His grace (Eph 2:1–10, John 3:16). We cannot, therefore, lessen the severity of one without changing the level of glittering truth in the other. Christ in the same breath contrasted the everlasting life of His sheep with the everlasting punishment of the goats (Matt 25:46), and that was among many such declarations by Christ of the coming judgment. He wished us to see the parallel clearly, and so we must strive to hear and see the force of His words.

When considering Hell, we do so beholding both the goodness and severity of God. We must deal with its severity as it is stated. We cannot demand clemency for the transgression from the holy throne of the righteous judge. We cannot declare that God has no right to cut off anyone. We cannot take the subject of Hell lightly or attempt to twist it to fit our sensitivities. Hell is the ultimate symbol of the severity of God's justice.

What is at stake is the character of God and the nature of reality. If we deny the severity of God we end up with a God that will not deal with evil. If we deny the severity of God, then we have given up all hope for justice. There is no reasonable person that would deny the reality of injustices and the fact that those injustices rarely, if ever, are corrected in this world. Many wicked oppressors will lay their head down in peace at their death. One may not want to call it sin or evil because it would unleash the terrorizing reality of God, but it gnaws at them. Give up on morality or admit that there is real justice beyond the grave. We are left with no God and no justice. Some form of impersonal law, like karma, judges nothing. The personal God of the Scriptures alone judges with the severity that matches the injustices. Emmanuel Kant reasoned that we cannot without contradiction conceive of God as a kindly judge, for that would make sin permissible. We must hold that He meets out punishment in accordance with the deeds that were done.[1] On this point, we must agree with Kant, even while rejecting his metaphysics. The severity of God is a necessary precondition to moral reasoning. If the evils of men are not brought to a place of accountability then morality and justice are but a mockery as concepts; niceties that have no relationship to the way things truly are.

To simply deny severity under the heading of God's love not only destroys the accounting of evil, but it also destroys the very concept of God's love. God's love is objective by nature. The denial of severity in God denies the ability or right of God to choose to set His love distinctly on any object. If there is no severity that may be exercised by God in the actual rejection of that which is repugnant to Him then no distinction can be made by God between the object of His love and His enemies. This blurring of categories is known as *universalism*, the idea that all people in all times are or will be made objects of God's love at some future time. If a man shakes his fist at God in continued unrepentant rebellion and hatred for

---

1. Immanuel Kant, *Lectures on Ethics*; Cambridge University Press, 1997.

God then God must save that one in the end. If such a one despises and without repentance wastes and destroys those God has made objects of His love the hands of God are universally bound from any exercise of ultimate judgment against those enemies. The "God is love and therefore, even our love of darkness is loved by Him," stance is the great error of the modern sexual revolution ideology. There can, in the scheme of universalism, be no real and final judgment. Such is contrary to the revealed truth of Scriptures that declare that God is angry against the sinner (Ps 7:11), hates the sinner (Ps 5:5, 11:5), will repay those that hate Him (Deut 7:10), and in a final and complete way bring the severity of His judgment upon those that have hated the objects of His love (Matt 25:31–46).

God must, under the false view of universalism, love His enemies *and* their deeds. There is a sense that God loves those who were enemies but by grace have repented. And there is a general truth that God extends kindness in this present world to both good and evil people. But God is indeed the enemy of those that hate Him and He hates their deeds. People do not consider themselves haters of God (not even atheists who see themselves as rejecting only a non-existent concept). But they love their sin that opposes God and hate His servants that seek to warn them of their error. The prophets of God are always mocked and killed in every age. Those not for Christ are against Him (Matt 12:30).

But love rejoices not in iniquity but in truth (I Cor 13:6, 7). That is most true of perfect, divine love. To love truth and righteousness, which is the ontologically necessary truth of the nature of God that makes the existence of justice possible in the created order, is to hate lies and iniquity. Severity in God is that which allows Him in love to "sever," or cut away from Himself, that which is contrary to His truth and righteousness. It is, in the same vein of truth, that which allows God to "sever" from His loved ones the things that are not in accordance with their good. The love of a father will smash the head of the poisonous serpent crawling in the children's playground.

Many clear Scriptural metaphors can be called forth to demonstrate that love demands severity. The metaphor of the parent as already stated above is immediately invoked in our thoughts. The father that will not discipline his child, to correct with some severity those things that are harmful to the child, does not love that child (Prov 13:24). As a child, my rebellious disruptions in church were marked by the furrowed brow and intense stare of my father's disapproval. I knew them to be signs of severity that

4

corrected my behavior. I look back at them now as tokens of love; a love that dealt severely with the harmful sinfulness in me. But back then, sinful rebellion felt severity come to fruition by the leather strap. A loving parent would also hate those that seek to harm their children. A bear robbed of her young would deal in severity with the ones posing a danger to her cubs (Prov 17:12).

A more apt metaphor would be a king that will not gather out of his kingdom those things that destroy and offend that kingdom. Such a king does not care about the kingdom or its citizens (Matt 13:41). A good king must hate the enemy. And he must despise those that remain enemies out of love for his kingdom and its true citizens. This is the light by which we understand the imprecatory psalms. A good king (as opposed to the modern politician) hates the enemies of his kingdom due to his love for its citizens. We know that we have rejoiced politically with the destruction of our national enemies. How much more shall our God delight in the destruction of His enemies and ours, and we share in that rejoicing.

One of the greatest metaphors for the doctrine of righteous severity comes from the lips of our Lord, as recorded by Matthew in his eighteenth chapter. This metaphor brings us closer to the reality of our subject, the Hell of final judgment. The metaphor is encapsulated in these words that are more fully explained in the broader text, "But whoso shall offend one of these little ones which believe in me, it were better for him that a millstone were hanged about his neck, and that he were drowned in the depth of the sea. . . ." (Matt 18:6) Before we understand the direction of the metaphor and the ominous words "better for him," which draws toward the tight analogy of God's severe and final judgment, we must ask ourselves what the metaphor is. In the second verse, Jesus brought a small child to Himself, a *paidion*, between infancy and seven years of age. At this age, the child is in training, unable to decide for themself, dependent on the leading and learning of others, and unable to defend or protect itself in the least. According to Christ, the reality that the metaphor reaches toward is that those that believe upon Christ are under the rule of His kingdom. They are objects of His love and care (Matt 18:3–5, 10–11). Christ is received of such and cares that such are received by others, for they are His own.

To this metaphor is added a despised enemy, one that would go about to harm such a little one. Those who despise the Gospel and also despise those that carry it (either directly in hatred or indirectly in indifference) are in view here, for they teach others to despise God by their lives. These enemies are introduced with a Greek subjunctive (a possible reality) as those that might go about to cause the little ones to stumble or fall or also might scandalize (*skandalizó*) the little ones.

People in our present culture still understand this metaphor. We are angry when we hear of vulnerable children being physically or sexually harmed by the intentional acts of depraved adults. Working in the field of child protection, nothing drew more righteous anger than the cases of child rape. We are more than ready to call down upon the heads of such perpetrators the most violent Anathemas. If such are convicted, they must be held in some form of protective custody to keep them from being harmed in jail by other criminals who also hold such in the highest contempt.

Our conscience tells us that severity is needed. Again, when working child protection cases, we often interviewed alleged sexual abuse perpetrators in conjunction with law enforcement. Inevitably, the officer asked, "What do you think should happen to someone who did something like this?" The question is intended to reveal a guilty conscience. The natural answer of one unfettered by a guilty conscience would be severe against the evil. The guilty conscience however would be light. Why? Because the clean conscience believes in the need of severe judgment to answer the reality of the evil work. Those who deny Hell are always in danger of also denying the reality of punishable evil in this world.

To this absolute need of severity, Christ gives the metaphor of the millstone being hung around the enemy's neck. Literally, it was a stone that, due to its size, was moved by a horse or a donkey. And then the enemy would be cast into the middle of Sea. Now the reality reaches toward those of the world, enemies of the kingdom of Christ and the little ones who believe upon Him (Matt 18:7).

The millstone dragging those who offend against little children down to the depths of the Sea, and drowning them violently is appropriate and righteous judgment. It answers well to the consciences of us all. But that is the metaphor for those in the world who are enemies of the rightful King of kings and haters of those under His rule. Such an end is not severe enough for His enemies, and the millstone would be "better than" the severity that awaits them. In the same vein, Christ warned that it would be "more tolerable" for the men of Sodom than for those that saw the works of Christ and rejected Him (Matt 11:20–24).

What is the reality which is drawn forward by the metaphor? It is fearful enough that Christ warns them that if it took them severing their hand,

PART 1 | THE SEVERITY OF GOD

foot, or right eye, then that would be a reasonable length to go to in order to escape this fate (Matt 18:8,9). What would be a fearful enough fate to cause you to begin to cut your own foot off in order to escape it? When you grasp that, then you begin to ascertain what God intends for you in His final judgment, absent you obtaining His mercy now. To escape such is to enter into life. To be subject to the severity is to be cast into eternal fire; fire that is without end (Matt 18:8).

The reality reached by the metaphor is the ultimate expression of the righteous and holy severity of God. It was given a symbolic name by Christ, the Gehenna of fire. We will unpack this symbolic language later under a different heading. For now, Gehenna is the name given to the place in the valley outside of the city of Jerusalem where the fire burned up the waste. It was fitting to draw people's minds to the severity of God's final judgment by use of such a name. Gehenna is where things worthy of the waste pile were committed.

The Psalmist described the only appropriate response to such a God. "My flesh trembles for fear of thee; and I am afraid of thy judgments." (Ps 119:120) There is no refuge in the false hope of universalism. There is finality in the severity of God. The reality of God's law demands the end of those who despise, "the riches of [God's] goodness and forbearance and longsuffering. . ." which God uses to lead them to repentance while He might be found (Rom 2:4). To them the threatening of severity is declared, "wrath against the day of wrath and revelation of the righteous judgment of God. . . ." (Rom 2:5) They will receive according to their deeds in true justice, "indignation and wrath, tribulation and anguish. . . ." (Rom 2:6–9) They will, as workers of iniquity, be told by Christ to forever depart from Him (Matt 7:23).

The King of kings will deal in severity with the enemies of His rule. Going back to the text of Paul, God's severity is the truth of history. We have seen the rule of God brought to bear on His enemies in the pages of history. The house of Israel was left desolate for despising its Lord (Matt 23:38). The Canaanites were utterly given over to the sword. The same fate will be brought to bear on nations of the Gentiles that fulfill that same pattern (Rom 11:21). Jerusalem of old was given over to Babylon, who with maliciousness destroyed them. And in answer to Babylon's cruelty, God gave Babylon over to similar severe wrath. This God has made Sodom and its sister cities examples, real and historic, to His fiery wrath and eternal judgment (Jude 1:7).

7

Those are not the only examples accessible to us of the righteous existence of severity. God has put a sword in the hands of the state to judge right and wrong in the light of God's word and to bring fearful judgment against those who do evil. Though a forgotten truth in our lawless and perishing culture, we can still with a generational memory remember days where the murderer would be strapped to the chair and destroyed, and the great criminals would have ropes put around their neck and dropped violently to their death. It was a fearfully just end.

The last execution I remember was a serial murderer and rapist. However, I only remember it being spoken about, for it did not happen openly or speedily. As the severity of righteous judgment slips from our collective memory, we see the most wicked people emboldened and know intuitively that unless that severe sword is again wielded by the state under the influence of God's law, our culture will crumble. We know that the fearful truth of the severity of God is true, righteous, and necessary.

It is in that light that the doctrine of Hell is presented to us by our Lord in His word. Fear the One that can destroy both body and soul in Hell (Matt 10:28). With severity being passed out of our memory and the fear of God that it was supposed to teach us, we excuse ourselves in some delusion of universalism. When giving people the Gospel, my father used to ask them directly if they believed that they deserved Hell. Those who did not understand the Gospel would inevitably say that they did not deserve Hell and that they were not that bad. That is how he knew that they did not understand salvation and that he needed to again turn the conversation back to their need of Christ as a guilty sinner. The matter now is much worse, people believe somehow that Hell itself is an unjust concept. God help us as we navigate such a-moral philosophies.

Chapter 1

Hell Is a Representation of God's Wisdom and Goodness

"Verily I say unto you, It shall be more tolerable for the land of Sodom and Gomorrha in the day of judgment, than for that city"

MATTHEW 10:15

"And that servant, which knew his lord's will, and prepared not himself, neither did according to his will, shall be beaten with many stripes. But he that knew not, and did commit things worthy of stripes, shall be beaten with few stripes. For unto whomsoever much is given, of him shall be much required: and to whom men have committed much, of him they will ask the more"

LUKE 12:47–48

SOLOMON SOUGHT WISDOM FROM God in order to rule over the nation of Israel, and God gave him wisdom that surpassed the wisdom of all other earthly kings and kingdoms. That wisdom was exhibited first in his ability to wisely administer justice to the innocent and guilty in his kingdom. The quintessential example is the two women that came before him, one honest and the other dishonest, to lay claim on a living child. By his judgment he was able to discern the true and false by making the desires of the women's hearts manifest (I Kings 3:16–28). The guilt of one was made manifest by his judgment and the sincerity of the other was, as well.

Of course, Solomon was a type of a greater Son who is to rule over the kings of the earth and whose kingdom will have no end (Ps 2, 89, 145:13, Dan 4:3, II Pet 1:11). Christ identified Himself as that greater Son and said all judgment is delivered to Him as the Son (See Ps 2). "For the Father judges no man, but hath committed all judgment unto the Son: that all men should honor the Son, even as they honor the Father." (John 5:22) Solomon was the initial type of wisdom of the greater Son in judgment.

There are interesting parallels that can be seen between the rule of Solomon and the rule of Christ. David entrusted the judgment of his enemies to Solomon (I Kings 2). The judgment of bloody Joab was wisely meted out. And the treasonous guilt of Shimei was made apparent by his understanding. Not only was the judgment of the enemies laid at the feet of the wise son, but also the rewarding of the faithful such as the sons of Barzillai. Solomon was able to bring forth the right judgment of the wicked and the right reward to the just. This is what we trust in the hands of the greater Son, Jesus Christ. He can wisely judge the world and every individual in it. "For we must all appear before the judgment seat of Christ; that everyone may receive the things done in his body, according to that he hath done, whether it be good or bad." (II Cor 5:10)

Solomon was able to rightly bring to justice those who despised the kingdom and the former king. In essence, Solomon displayed wisdom by his ability to rightly compare and contrast and come to a right conclusion in judgment. He could discern men's intent and wisely choose a course of action. With this wisdom he wrote works of wisdom and built a kingdom that was the envy of the world. However, his ability to rightly judge would ultimately fail, for he was not good and, therefore, his wisdom was not perfectly exercised. His kingdom crumbled after his death and, outside of what God has preserved by inspiration and transmission, no lasting emblem remains of the glory of Solomon; not so much as one stone sitting upon another.

What we must consider about the subject of final judgment is that it is indeed the careful product of perfect judgment. If we cannot approach the subject with this simple faith, then we do not have the perfect God of the Scriptures as the object of our faith but rather, some man-made idol. Hell is seen in the light of the One who is far greater than Solomon and has adorned the whole world with more glory than Solomon could. "Consider the lilies of the field, how they grow; they toil not, neither do they spin: And yet I say unto you, that even Solomon in all his glory was not arrayed like one of these." (Matt 6:28, 29) The wisdom of the one that will judge all things is infinite wisdom and cannot be compared with the wisdom of the wisest men, like Solomon. Final judgment flows from that. And unlike Solomon, it comes from a source that is perfectly good, as well. It comes from perfect and unfailing wisdom and from moral perfection. The eyes of Christ will judge all things righteously, without any mixture of evil, and wisely, without any mixture of error.

Inevitably, honest concerns and objections about the doctrine of Hell are answered by these convictions about the character of God of whom the character of Christ is the expressed image. How can we object to His good and wise determined ends? It is not the judgment of fallible man but the infallible God from a perfect knowledge of all things and from perfectly pure motives that is represented by final judgment. It is judgment that is impeccable, without need of appeal, and perfect in every way. And when we wrestle with the issues of righteous severity we rest in the fact that we are speaking of a good God who is the sum and source of all wisdom and goodness. Judgment is safe here.

This is taken for granted by the biblical writers. As such, they present final judgment without a hint of embarrassment or controversy in all they say or even leave unsaid. Consider concerns from the objection of relative innocence as it relates to the doctrine of Hell. The doctrine of original sin tells us that all are guilty in Adam (Rom 5:12–14). All are born sinful and already under condemnation (John 3:18). God has shown in this temporal world that He may in grace count a child innocent (Deut 1:39), or in justice count them guilty (I Sam 15:3). As such, what does that mean for the case in which an infant dies, either a child of faithful believers or the child of the unbelieving? The truth of the doctrine of original sin cannot be skirted when speaking with either the unbelieving or the believing. The infant was a sinner under condemnation. This leaves a gap in understanding that the biblical writers and the God they revealed saw no need to explain. That is, the question is left unanswered, "What happens when an infant dies?"

What can we do but turn to the nature of the good and wise Judge. There is no direct text of Scripture that is able to say to either the believing or unbelieving parent that their infant is indeed with God. But a comfort can be given to the believing that the unbelieving are unable to receive. The believing can receive by way of comfort, a belief that the Judge of all the earth will do right in His judgment. That is, He will do in judgment what is in accordance with His good and wise nature (Gen 18:25, Luke 12:3). That same God that had mercy on the believing parent through Christ is able to do so with their child. Their God is a good God and a wise God, full of compassion and mercy (Ps 145:8, 9). They can trust in Him, even with this deep fear related to relative innocence. In other words, they can trust that the God who saved them by grace alone may so choose to save their infant by that same grace. Therefore, men like David could say in faith that when his child died, he would one day be able to go where the baby had gone (II Sam 12:23). This is only an existential crisis for one who refuses faith in the God of the Scriptures.

A similar objection might be made by considering an older child or even an adult who has little understanding of the greatness of their sin and need of Christ. There is no need to weave an ad hoc doctrine of the age of accountability, which tends to deny the doctrine of original sin, or rest on some guessing game about whether they had sufficient understanding. The same trust we have in the all-wise and all-good God to rightly judge in the case of the infant, we do so here also. The gaps in revealed truth on these topics (to answer in any affirmative or dissenting opinions) is filled rather with our faith in the knowledge of our God revealed. He is good and wise and will choose, or elect, from that nature. And He will finally judge from that same truth. We will in the end be able to say, "our God has done all things well!" What better place can we rest than the revealed truth of the goodness of our God.

What we know with certainty is that the doctrine of Hell, that is the final judgment, is the product of wise judgment and deliberation. Hence, the Scriptures use the word judgment to speak of its enactment (II Tim 4:1). Consider specifically the judgment of the wicked servant who hid the talent of his lord. The servant was judged by his lord in accordance with the knowledge that he had of the nature and character of his lord, even a faulty knowledge (Matt 25:24–27). That was the basis of his final judgment and stands, according to Christ, as an emblem of the judgment to come upon all. "For unto every one that hath shall be given, and he shall have abundance: but from him that hath not shall be taken away even that which he hath. And cast ye the unprofitable servant into outer darkness: there shall be weeping and gnashing of teeth." (Matt 25:29, 30) Wisdom guides the final judgment; perfect wisdom. Goodness guides it; perfect goodness.

Christ brings this idea to bare specifically in several passages that merit a closer look here. In the context of the Son coming to judge the world, Christ said:

"And that servant, which knew his lord's will, and prepared not himself, neither did according to his will, shall be beaten with many stripes. But he that knew not, and did commit things worthy of stripes, shall be beaten with few stripes. For unto whomsoever much is given, of him shall be much required: and to whom men have committed much, of him they will ask the more." Luke 12:47, 48

We noted what was marked above already. The judgment is based on a perfect knowledge of what the servant knew to be true. Also, there is a perfect knowledge of the works that flowed from that knowledge. Each servant stood in a differing relationship to the will of God. From that perfect evaluation of each servant's case, the wisdom of the Judge is exercised to give final judgment to each.

That wisdom is presented to us in the use of comparative adjectives that show the real and perfect comparing and contrasting of each case. The punishment differs. For some it is described as "many" (*polus*). For others it is described as "few" (*oligos*). And this reflects a principle that underpins the final judgment. God will require from all at the final judgment that which is in accordance with what they have been given. God will not exact a disproportionate judgment on anyone. If you have been given little knowledge, little opportunity, little experience of grace, then our Lord will or rather has already discerned it. But if you are among those that have been given more, the all-wise God knows and will judge according to His perfectly good standard.

This is not intended to be a comfort to most that hear or read these words. Likely, it is not a comfort to any, unless they use it as a false comfort. It is normal for the fallen sinner to attempt to minimize their sinfulness and the vast amount of grace and mercy they have been given. But as we step back and view how our Lord will exercise His final judgment with that perfect wisdom, we can, in faith, rest all that we believe about Hell in that. He will do wisely when He punishes the sinner. If that judgment belonged to a fallible man or even a created angel, we would rightly doubt its wisdom. But we cannot do so here.

God also knows the level of our ignorance as it relates to our guilt. A servant is responsible to know the will of his master but may by negligence not know it. For this cause, ignorance is never and will never be an effectual plea. However, our wise God can judge even the liability of our ignorance. Ignorance still needs atonement (Lev 4). How much more when negligence and sinfulness inform that ignorance? Christ knows if we knew of potential danger but ignored it (Ex 21:28–32). He knows whether or not we hid our eyes from doing good (Deut 22:1–4). He knows whether we could have done otherwise (Ex 22:2). There is nothing about our character that God will not know in His judgment and take account of when He considers our liability.

Another example is when Christ said, "It shall be more tolerable for the land of Sodom and Gomorrah in the day of judgment, than for that city [which will not receive His messengers]" (Matt 10:15, Mark 6:11, Luke 10:12), and "It shall be more tolerable for Tyre and Sidon at the day of judgment than for you [who believed not nor repented when seeing the work of Christ]." (Matt 11:21–24, Luke 10:13–16) A comparative adjective again is used to demonstrate the exercise of perfect wisdom in final judgment. For some it will be "more tolerable" (*anektoteros*). As such, we ascertain that it will be worse for others based on the power of our God to ascertain the truth of what is truly merited. The men of Sodom will yet be judged in the future, and when they are raised in that judgment their fate will, for lack of a better term, be mixed with more of God's mercy than God's judgment of others who have been given more. Why is this? It is because the wisdom and knowledge of the Judge includes knowledge of what might have been. God knows all counterfactual or subjunctive facts. This is because He created each creature; He knows them. Those who have heard the Gospel and rejected it, not repenting, will have less mixture of mercy in their judgment than the men of Sodom. That was specifically true of those who saw the miracles of Christ and heard His words, but it created a broader principle that applies to all.

We can then rest in the truth that the nature of the wisdom of the Judge of all has such intimate knowledge of each of the creatures that He created that He knows every possible fact. Thus, our Lord makes perfect judgment of every creature. There will be no rock for the guilty to hide under and no consideration that the Judge of all will not take into account when He judges the living and the dead. He alone can judge the true weight of guilt.

And such is what is declared of His judgment. "But the Lord shall endure for ever: he hath prepared his throne for judgment. And he shall judge the world in righteousness, he shall minister judgment to the people in uprightness." (Ps 9:8) Therefore, even in his sin, David said that God's judgment is justified against him (Ps 51:4). Again, "O let the nations be glad and sing for joy: for thou shalt judge the people righteously, and govern the nations upon earth." (Ps 67:4, 96:10) And also, "[the Lord] cometh to judge the earth: with righteousness shall he judge the world, and the people with equity." (Ps 98:9) And in the end, we can be assured that His judgment will be right, and we will rejoice in it with marvel, "Thou art righteous, O Lord, which art, and wast, and shalt be, because thou hast judged thus." (Rev 16:5)

For a final example of the existence of wisdom in the final judgment there is also the case of the Pharisees. Christ declared, "Woe unto you, scribes and Pharisees, hypocrites! For ye devour widows' houses, and for a pretense make long prayer: therefore, ye shall receive the greater damnation." (Matt 23:14, Mark 12:40, Luke 20:47)[1] This considers not just the knowledge taken into account in deliberation but the final decision made; the final sentencing, the damnation or condemnation, the measurement of accountability, and the final decision of their liability. His wisdom is displayed in both the conviction and sentencing of the sinner. The same compare and contrast language is given to show the exercise of wisdom in its final product. The debate may be enflamed here whether the "greater" damnation refers to intensity of punishment or its duration (conditional mortality, a topic that will be taken up later), but the text does not answer that question, nor does it attempt to. The point here is that every aggravating circumstance is weighed by the wisdom of God in the final sentence. For some there will be more abundance (*perissos*) of condemnation. Some will be judged lightly, while others with greater guilt will be judged with greater severity. It is wisdom and goodness in perfection that informs the final judgment of all.

One warning should be observed. These comparisons are not meant to lead us to a structural view of Hell, as a tiered system, as in Dante's *Inferno*. And they are not meant to serve as a catalyst to teach specific forms of lesser punishments not in accordance with what the Scriptures teach, such as a purgatory-like universalist teaching of duration, releasing all eventually into heaven. The doctrine of Hell as declared by Christ is still meant to be as fearful for the ignorant and less liable as it is for the worst among us. These comparisons of severity draw our attention instead to the wisdom of our Lord. There may be a sinner that reads this that will be told one day that it will be worse for them. This ought to make the reader fear.

We lack wisdom to judge ourselves or anyone else rightly, for we are apt to think our guilt a light thing, or to judge more harshly the guilt of

---

1. Admittedly, older manuscripts do not contain this text in Matthew but do so in the synoptic references.

those around us, for we often consider them unmercifully. But God does not see with our eyes. He sees what each of us really are. The guilty have reason to fear even more at these applications of wisdom. He knows the true extent of the harm your sin has caused to others and the intent in your heart. Our covering of religion does not fool Him. "For there is nothing covered, that shall not be revealed; neither hid, that shall not be known." (Luke 12:2)

The only warranted way to approach the topic of Hell is with the infinite wisdom of such a Judge in mind. Inserting our own opinions or feelings is to try to apply an inferior wisdom to the final judgment. Whatever scenarios or objections about Hell people maintain, they are met first by our faith in His wisdom. It is part of the revelation about Hell that it is drawn from His exercise of wisdom, and therefore, we will be able to say in the end that He did all things well and will marvel at His judgment. "The Lord knows how to deliver the godly out of temptations and to reserve the unjust unto the day of judgment to be punished. . . ." (II Pet 2:9) The first Psalm has this very truth at its core, the Lord recognizes the righteous and the wicked and knows their proper end (Ps 1). In His wisdom and goodness He has a place determined for both.

But the wisdom of God is not vindictive or cunning. His wisdom is good, and His goodness is wise. He is a good God that judges men wisely and a wise God that judges men rightly. We must trust in the wisdom of a good God when contemplating His final judgment. "He is the Rock, his work is perfect: for all his ways are judgment: a God of truth and without iniquity, just and right is he." (Deut 32:4) Flawed and iniquitous men are completely incapable of judging the judgment of the Ultimate and Good Judge.

We must qualify the meaning of good as it applies to the character of God. It is not the same as saying that God does good. He does good to the evil and to the good in this present world (Matt 5:45). The rain and sunshine come to all as good things experienced in this life. To do good flows from a good nature. God being good is what was meant by Christ when He said there is one that is good, which is God (Mark 10:18). In that context, Christ desired to set up a comparison between the true nature of goodness as compared to a man who believed himself to be good. It was revealed in that context that the man was not good at all when compared to divine goodness. There are limits to the moral goodness of man but there are no limits to the moral perfection of God. He will do good and do right in His judgment and in all He does. His goodness reveals our guilt and assures us that He will not distribute judgment contrary to that goodness. His judgment will be fair, and it will be just. It will neither be too light, nor too heavy in each individual case. His ways are not unequal. That is a designation that belongs properly to an unrighteous man (Ezek 18:25).

On this basis, we do not separate the goodness of God from His final judgment. His goodness is what is despised in the rejection of His presently extended mercy (Rom 2:3, 4). Because He is good, He leads men to repentance. A good king makes His laws and expectations known by posting them openly and allowing opportunity to all to conform to his norm. If any sin ignorantly, they still are liable, for they could have and should have sought to know their master's will. God has made His expressed will known because He is good. His law has gone out. His mercy has been extended. But in the end, He will sit in judgment. As a good Judge, He cannot clear the guilty (Ex 34:7). He will not wink at evil nor pervert His justice. He will not be bribed or be favorable to certain groups or persons (Rom 2:11). The judgment of all will come and none can expect either leniency or undue punishment. His wise judgment will be good.

Thus, His judgment will not fail to vindicate the righteous and punish the guilty. In that light, we see the repeated parables of Christ regarding the final judgment which will be at the end of the world. There the wise God will show that He fully knows the difference between those who are good (the wheat and the good fish) and those who are evil (the tares and the evil fish). He will in His goodness do with them as is proper to their nature. He will gather the good into good places and the evil into places proper to them. And what is the reality thus described behind the allegories of the fisherman and the harvester? "The Son of man shall send forth his angels, and they shall gather out of his kingdom all things that offend, and them which do iniquity; And shall cast them into a furnace of fire: there shall be wailing and gnashing of teeth." (Matt 13:41, 42) So again, the allegory is drawn to its reality, "So shall it be at the end of the world: the angels shall come forth, and sever the wicked from among the just, and shall cast them into the furnace of fire: there shall be wailing and gnashing of teeth." (Matt 13:50, 51)

Goodness and Wisdom produce this judgment. The same is clearly brought forth in the parable of the sheep and goats. There the allegory points to the activities of our God in the reality of His judgment. In His wisdom, He gathers all and separates them. In His goodness, He receives the righteous and rejects those who are not righteous. In the end, the weight of the reality of this wise and good judgment falls, "these [the unrighteous] shall go away into everlasting punishment: but the righteous into life eternal." (Matt 25:46) Each will, by His wise and good judgment, know themselves to be rightly judged.

The thrust of this line of thought is that our Lord is not like us in judgment. He is the perfect evaluator of all things. Our Lord once was able to weigh between Pilate and the elders of the people who betrayed Him. He was able to say that one had the "greater sin" and therefore had merited the greater punishment (John 19:11). Everyone who stands before the Judge of all stands before the one who knows the full extent of their guilt, and they will know what has truly been merited by their sin. There will not be a mistake or injustice. The judgment will be good and wise. No one else can or will be entrusted with the final judgment but the Son, and it rests safely there. Where our judgment is flawed, His judgment cannot be accused of folly or injustice. Fear Him! One day, the Holy Goodness of His character will cause all creation to flee (Rev 20:11, 12). He will sit on a great white throne. One day, His wisdom will be fully displayed as He has preserved all knowledge (Prov 22:12). Those books will be opened, and all will be judged by His perfect wisdom. From that flows the doctrine of Hell.

Chapter 2

The Doctrine of Hell Will Venerate God's Justice

"Knowing this, that the law is not made for a righteous man, but for the lawless and disobedient. . . ."

I TIMOTHY 1:9

"Now we know that what things soever the law saith, it saith to them who are under the law: that every mouth may be stopped, and all the world may become guilty before God."

ROMANS 3:19

UNDERSTANDING THE NATURE OF law, its purpose and importance in our time, is the most difficult matter of biblical interpretation. All Christians must wrestle with this theological reality: Christ has come and has accomplished "something" in time and as a result, "some things" are now different. The clause that states that Christ accomplished "something" is where the Christian faith lies, and it lies on sturdy ground. That ground will yet be explored later when the salvation of the believer from sin and God's righteous wrath is explored. For now, by way of summary, let us just say that any good news to be entertained or proclaimed comes under the heading of what Christ has accomplished.

The law of and by itself offers no good news to the guilty sinner. David could delight in the law of God as a result of his covenantal hope (Ps 89).

David could only tremble under the law as a guilty sinner (Ps 51). Related to that good news is the result clause, "some things" are now different. Here is where practical theology lies. It introduces the conundrum of the law and the question of the applicability of the law today. The practical application of God's law is what we seek.

The argument by some would be that since Christ has fulfilled the law of sin utterly, that He has saved all things and all people from the law. This argument states that the law is no longer relevant. Such a view is championed by universalists. Such a heretical thought springs from an over-interpretation of Gospel truths (Christ died for all, Christ is the proprietary atonement for the world, in Christ all shall be made alive, Christ has made us free from the law, etc.—themes we must return to at a later point as this conversation unfolds). From such sentiments springs doctrines of antinomian sentiments that remove definite categories of right and wrong and any sense of duty and obedience toward God.

Sin is a reality still, and the law gives the knowledge of sin (Rom 3:20). Such is the immediate role of the law. Sin is a transgression of the law (I John 3:4). The law serves to make us guilty as sinners instead of being sinners without guilt. It was a repugnant thought to Paul for Christian doctrine to be antinomian. In Romans 6:12 he says, "What shall we say then? Shall we continue in sin, that grace may abound? God forbid. How shall we, that are dead to sin, live any longer therein?" May such a thought never be entertained!

From this heresy also springs further rhetoric from universalism that denies the final judgment and final condemnation of any, for it is argued that if Christ died for all, then all are saved and no one will come into condemnation. Christ, however, taught that men are condemned already, and many will be raised to the resurrection of damnation (John 3:18, 5:29). It is, according to Paul, those who walk in the Spirit that shall not come into condemnation (Rom 8:1–4). So says Christ (John 5:24). There is no universal salvation from condemnation.

It is this biblical language of condemnation that speaks of the influence of the law. The fact that Christ has accomplished something and now things are different is a sound observation of biblical data. Even the instances pointed out above are general witnesses to that truth that must be understood in the light of the whole Scripture. This is the theological principle of continuity/discontinuity between the Old and New Covenants. This principle is the simple recognition that there are things between the law and Gospel that are the same and there are things that are different. The law is not destroyed but fulfilled, and the commandments have yet to be taught (I Tim 1:9–11, Matt 5:17–20). Christians are not a people without law but are a people saved from its condemnation (I Cor 9:21).

Theologians have attempted to describe continuity/discontinuity in various ways and each of us are limited by our own fallible capacity to be honest and consistent with the Old and the New Testaments. We know what we cannot do with the result clause. We cannot insert the word "everything" (i.e., everything is now different) as if the law of God is now irrelevant, things like adultery are now acceptable for the Christian, or the law says nothing about our moral and civil spheres. Types of the atonement and examples of obedience or disobedience still teach us and have relevance (Rom 15:4, I Cor 10:6, see whole book of Hebrews). But so do direct commands, for they tell us directly what sin is for which atonement is needed. To say that the Old Covenant is irrelevant is the extreme form of antinomianism, and it is contrary to the New Covenant.

We also cannot insert the word "nothing" as if the demands of the law are completely unaffected in their practice and, by consequence, Christ has accomplished nothing (i.e., nothing is changed and we still need a sacrifice, a priest, an altar, etc.—this is also contrary to the New Covenant). This latter idea must be taken up at a later time when we consider the salvation of God.

Right now, let us settle on this observation. The Law of God speaks with the same absolute moral authority that it always has spoken with. It is the voice of God speaking (Rom 3:19). Jude warned that there would be those creeping into the church who attempt to change the grace of God into wantonness and unrestrained behavior (*aselgeia*). They went about teaching that the grace of the Gospel removed any restraint of the law of God on behavior. Jude stated that the condemnation of such teachers has already been designated (Jude 1:4, John 3:18, 19). They will be judged with severity. To dismiss the reality of sin and its inseparable relationship to God's law is unbiblical and dishonest and is indicative of a heart hardened against God's grace.

Sin is lawlessness; it transgresses God's commands (I John 3:4), and those who are of God shun the practice of sin (I John 3:9). The law stands then as the moral standard by which we are judged. It represents to us the righteousness of God Himself, and when we stand before our God it will be that which confirms our guilt and the rightness of His judgment against the lawless. In other words, the law is that which is given by God that makes us accountable and liable before God. Whatever discontinuity is graciously given between the law and the Gospel, the law remains the standard by which we are judged. The standard of revealed righteousness is the certain continuity of the Scriptures.

In the end, the works of men will be judged by the law of God. This is the very sense of the Great White Throne judgment (Rev 20:11–15). All the dead (meaning the lost) will stand before God the Son (John 5:22–29). It is there, at this final judgment, that it says, "the books were opened. . . and the dead [i.e., the lost] were judged out of those things which were written in the books, according to their works. . . . And they were judged every man according to their works." (Rev 20:12, 13) Their works will be judged by what is contained in the books. There is not just an exhaustive remembrance of the works done by all that is brought up by the imagery of these books (Mal 3:16), but there is also the idea of the books producing a known standard by which those works will be compared. Their judgment comes out of or from the books.

The dead will be judged by those things that stand written by God. And it is a standard that is known by all, or at least should be known if one is not neglectful in their duty. None of the lost will be able to deny the truth contained in the books. Those who have never read them will show in their conscience that they are the true standard (Rom 2:14). The moral imperatives revealed by the law, the prophets, and the apostles will yet be a witness against the sins and evil works of men. Despite all philosophical and theological attempts to define away sin as a real concept and relegate the law to some categorical status of irrelevance, in the end all will have to contend with the law of God. The full weight of what James said, that to offend in one point makes one guilty of all, will be laid bare before the guilty (James 2:10). The law will be held up as the leveling tool that shows the crookedness of sinful humanity and from it declares their guilt and just condemnation.

Paul, in recognition of the continuity/discontinuity of the law since the advent of Christ, recognized that there was a right and wrong (lawful and unlawful) use of the law (I Tim 1:8). There are many possible ways that the law could be used unlawfully or wrongly (contrary to its intended end): as a means of justification or sanctification, as an attempt to re-establish what Christ has fulfilled and finished, as an esoteric and gnostic rubric for hidden knowledge, etc. The unlawful use of the law is beyond the scope of this present conversation. Paul, in that same context established a right and lawful use of the law since the advent of Christ. Of the law, which is good, he said:

> ". . . [It] is not made for a righteous man, but for the lawless and disobedient, for the ungodly and for sinners, for unholy and profane, for murderers of fathers and murderers of mothers, for manslayers, For whoremongers,[1] for them that defile themselves with mankind,[2] for men-stealers, for liars, for perjured persons, and if there be any other thing that is contrary to sound doctrine. . . ." I Timothy 1:9, 10

The law is presently enacted, appointed, or set in place (*keimai*) to show man their sin, whether that be in the sphere of government, family, or the individual conscience. It shows all the sinfulness of their sin right now in the present evil world and intends to turn them from it to Christ, who is the end or goal of the law (Rom 10:4). Paul elsewhere stated that the law made it known to him that lust was evil by declaring, as a holy word from God, "thou shalt not covet." (Rom 7:7) The law then is the holy and good voice of God still speaking to sinful men that their deeds are evil. It is a voice that demands repentance now and will yet be a voice heard at the final judgment when the books are opened. All are responsible to study it and to learn what pleases their Lord. All areas of our life are under His Lordship and command.

The law has a kind or benevolent use now to show the people their sins and lead to repentance. It will have a final voice at the judgment as it justifies the severity of God's condemnation of the sinner who would not repent. The law now speaks of our lost condition and need of salvation. This lost condition is the very thing that men wish to deny and they, therefore, hate the witness of the law. The desire is to either claim that one is "basically good" (a Pelagian view of humanity) or at least "not that bad" (a semi-Pelagian view of humanity). These are admittedly simple summaries of these views, but they are accurate summaries and are corrected by a sound view of God's law.

The law stands up as a present witness against these unbiblical views of anthropology. It tells each of us that we are part of a completely lost humanity, and as such, we are rebels and enemies against God who is over us.

1. *pornos*, the sexually immoral.

2. *arsenokoites*, same sex sexual relationship, a male with another male in bed, see LXX parallel from Lev 18:22.

We are a fallen race of sinners that, therefore, do sinful things. Absent the grace and mercy of God, we are unable to do righteous deeds and, therefore, unable to reconcile ourselves to our Lord whose commandments we have despised. We will address the subject of freewill and whether man is capable of responding to the mercy of God extended to them when we deal with the matter of salvation. For now, we will just focus on the lost condition of man, biblical anthropology.

The law of God answers the pressing questions. How lost are we? How guilty are we before our God? How deserving of the fullness of God's wrath are we? The Pelagian says we are not lost at all, but by our free-will acts we may perfect ourselves and come to God by our own righteousness. It teaches that we are born sinless and may maintain and achieve perfection and salvation on our own. If asked, the Pelagian would say, "I've kept the commandments and have done good things. God will accept me because I am a good person." They say all of this, knowing that all attempts at perfecting oneself fails. For some reason, they cannot keep from sinning.

The semi-Pelagian may admit that we are part of a fallen race and may even do bad things, but we are still able to respond to the light we have and will be judged in accordance with that. They might say, "I have made some mistakes, but I have tried my best, and when God judges me He will see that and have mercy." They say all of this knowing that they have not done enough good and have not responded to available light.

Obviously, the above is a truncated and incomplete representation of Pelagian and semi-Pelagian views which encompass broader implications to the subjects of original sin, free-will, and divine sovereignty. And the deeper problems with those unbiblical philosophies lie in those spheres. But this truncated representation provides a good summary of how people view their relationship with God, His law, and their standing before God in that light. Depending partially or totally on the ability of self, they approach God believing they may, as such, have salvation. Paul offered the decisive repudiation of such conclusions. How guilty and how lost are we? Paul says we are totally guilty and totally fallen.

We are, as Sproul would have said, cosmic rebels. We are sinners by nature and by choice. We are children of wrath by our nature, born in a sinful condition of heart that is opposed to the authority of God (Eph 2:1–3). We entered the world already sinners against a holy and righteous Judge and are already guilty. This is the sense that Christ gave when He said that we are "condemned already." (John 3:18) We were in Adam when he received the command and the promise that the wages of sin is death. We were in Adam when he allowed the entertainment of thoughts that God's authority could be doubted, questioned, and challenged by man's autonomous arbitration and reasoning (Gen 3:1–6, Rom 5:12–18). We were in Adam when he rebelled, and the righteous sentence of death fell. In Adam all have died already (I Cor 15:22). We come into this world dead in our sins (Eph 2:1). We were in Adam when he realized the shamefulness of his condition and hid from God in his defiled conscience.

There is a reason why the "Keep Off the Grass" sign immediately works in each of our hearts and minds the desire to transgress the command. We, in Adam, declared that we are our own gods. And as such, we are condemned. We are God's enemies, filthy and guilty and suitable for the severity of His judgment. It is only the grace of God and His longsuffering that allows us to breathe His air. But the time will come when God will impute to the lost man their sin. Or as Paul summed up; "through the offense of one many be dead. . . ," "the judgment was by one to condemnation. . . ," "by one man's offense death reigned by one. . . ," "by the offense of one judgment came upon all men to condemnation. . . ," and "by one man's disobedience many were made sinners. . . ." (Rom 5:14–19) This is what we are by nature.

Now, our fruit reveals our roots, and our fruits are rotten. Humanity as a whole, according to Paul, stands in the lofty position of knowing God of having the witness of God in us, and beholding His works in this world (Rom 1:18–20). But we know God in disobedience and hate that knowledge. Like Adam, we hide from God who is clearly seen and known. Being helped with the abundant revelation of God to clearly see, specifically the warning of His judgment and wrath, man will spit at God, refusing to give Him glory and thanks, and declaring themselves to be autonomous from Him in wisdom, purposefully distorting and reducing God to a creature like themselves or even less, dishonoring their bodies with sexual immorality and perversion, perverting God's truth, and worshiping His creation instead of Him (Rom 1:21–28).

Mankind in his fallen state hates God and runs swiftly into all that opposes the one true God they pretend is not there. So Paul paints the picture of the depraved nature of the enemies of God.

> "Being filled with all unrighteousness, fornication, wickedness, covetousness, maliciousness; full of envy, murder, debate, deceit, malignity; whisperers, backbiters, haters of God, despiteful,

proud, boasters, inventors of evil things, disobedient to parents, Without understanding, covenant-breakers, without natural affection, implacable, unmerciful: Who knowing the judgment of God, that they which commit such things are worthy of death, not only do the same, but have pleasure in them that do them." Romans 1:29–32

We are filled with all this. We know God's righteous moral decrees but love to break them and love to be entertained by those who break them.

Religious inclinations make the fallen nature of man no better. It is the fig leaf covering that pretends that God cannot see the shame of our hidden deeds. So Paul spoke to the Jews who saw themselves as the possessors of God's law. The religious judge guilt in others that they excuse in themselves, reject the tug of God to turn from unrighteousness, hear God but refuse to do what He has spoken, and go about (being confident in our own goodness and telling others to reject lawlessness) committing blasphemy and idolatry and sexual immorality. They hide behind a religious facade that neither atones for sin nor makes one righteous (Rom 2).

As such, all the advantages of the Jews were not to the end of salvation from sin and condemnation. They heard from God but refused to obey Him. When the books of the law are opened it will show what they, like the Gentiles, truly are. They, according to the Word, were not righteous, had no understanding, were not true seekers of God, were not keepers of God's way, were not furthering God's good ends, and were not doers of good things (Rom 3:1–18). What they saw themselves to be melted away in the face of honest analysis. Any cursory reading of the Old Covenant documents reveals this to be the case with the nation of Israel. Instead of being what they should have been, they were positively wicked. The true history of Jerusalem and Samaria is that of corruption, cursing, deceit, and destruction. They were not at peace with God and neither did they fear Him.

The word that Paul applies to the religious and irreligious alike, to the Jew and the Gentile, is the word inexcusable (*anapologétos*); being without an answer, defense, or apology. All wish to justify themselves. The heathen might say, "We were not at Sinai, we did not know." We learn to sin early in life and do so often. No one has to teach us. Adam, the father of us all, blamed the woman and his God for his sin. God, however, has said to the heathen that they are without excuse (Rom 1:20). Even if no one has read the revealed words of God's law to them, they know them. Every human being has a conscience, a knowledge of right and wrong, good and evil.

How do they know? They know because they live in God's world. They demonstrate that conscience individually and collectively in the exercise of law. They accuse others, justly or unjustly, of evil. They excuse themselves and their party by that same knowledge. They know that the Creator God has established a standard, and they know that the same God will visit them with wrath against all unrighteousness. Yet they run to evil, and like an adulterous woman they will partake of its fruit, wipe their mouths, and say they have done nothing wrong (Prov 30:20). The excusing of sin for them will end when they are confronted with the presence of the God that spoke His Word at the final judgment. So, the religious are equally, if not increasingly, inexcusable (Rom 2:1). Having actually heard the voice of God thunder from Sinai, they went about to likewise sin. They sin against greater light. And while they now go about to give excuses for themselves, they will one day also have no defense.

The reality of the judgment is the reality of the inexcusable nature of sin. That truth will there be manifest. Man now takes refuge in lies, either of a secular or religious nature. They do wrong and dismiss the reality of sin or diminish the exceeding sinfulness thereof. They believe that they can cover it with Pelagian or Semi-Pelagian excuses ("I am not a sinner" or "I am not that bad"). Paul highlights the inexcusable nature of what we all are with his terse description of final judgment.

> "Now we know that what things soever the law saith, it saith to them who are under the law: that every mouth may be stopped, and all the world may become guilty before God. Therefore, by the deeds of the law there shall no flesh be justified in his sight: for by the law is the knowledge of sin." Romans 3:19, 20

The law is presently speaking. All people are under its authority and jurisdiction. All people are guilty of falling short of its perfection but are instead totally in rebellion against it. They cannot then, when confronted with its reality, justify themselves. They will stand at the final reading of the law with no defense. They will stand at the bar of God's justice with full and perfect knowledge that they have sinned and are sinners. Their mouths will be stopped. They are guilty and will know it. They will be unable to say about their condemnation that it is unjust or that God is unjust in imputing their guilt to them. The guilty are those that go into Hell. Read that sentence again and let it sink in. It is the guilty that go to Hell. Every sinner that goes into Hell will do so fully convinced that it is right in the end.

And so, the purpose of the law is to make us guilty before God. For now, that is a potential blessing but at the final judgment it will become an irreversible curse. The reading of the law on that day, when the books are opened, will pierce men to their heart. The Gentile cannot appeal to anything in their philosophies to give a defense or to any power in their idols to hide them. The law will say to them irrevocably, "Guilty!" The Jew, or religious man, will find no loophole in any commandment to excuse them of their willful rebellion. Irrevocably, they will be found "Guilty!" The word used by Paul, which is translated guilty, is *hupodikos*. It means to be under judgment. It is a term for one that has lost their trial or suit before the bar of justice. It is not just one who is accused or indicted, but one that is convicted and sentenced justly, as well. They are those that are liable and now are fit for condemnation. This is the reality of God's final judgment. It needs to be meditated on soberly and honestly.

There is one great point to be remembered in our discussion on Hell. Whatever Hell is in its reality, it is a deserved reality. Hell is a symbol of God's justice and before one single soul is cast into it they will know without any excuse that they deserve to go there. Later, we will have the glorious opportunity to speak of imputed righteousness and God justifying and accounting the sinner righteous through Christ. It is the acquittal of the sinner by their justification before God. Hell is its opposite. It is the justification of the law of God alone as that which men should have obeyed but did not. It is the imputation of sin and guilt on the guilty sinner.

And as we go further into our understanding thereof, we should view ourselves in that light. When we stand before the perfect righteousness of God and His law, do we dream that we will be able to defend ourselves, our actions, our thoughts, our words, our plans, and our decisions? The time to hear the voice of God's word and law is now and not then. The gracious law now says to repent and leads us to Christ. If we will not hear that now, we must hear its guilty verdict then. How shall we escape the damnation of Hell?

Chapter 3

Hell Is a Revealed Truth of God to Be Believed

"It is a fearful thing to fall into the hands of the living God."

HEBREWS 10:31

"Vengeance is mine; I will repay, saith the Lord."

ROMANS 12:19

"And fear not them which kill the body, but are not able to kill the soul: but rather fear him which is able to destroy both soul and body in hell."

MATTHEW 10:28

THERE IS NO GREATER and more fundamental truth of morality than that man must believe his God. Truth is not created in the human mind and reality is not puddy for our individual minds to provide shape. Reality is created and decreed by God and our duty is to act in accordance with its truth. In that sense, we approach the subject of Hell as a matter of faith, that is, a matter of believing God. All knowledge is an exercise of faith, that is, all knowledge is justified true belief about something or another. What we know about Hell is either a belief that is true, being justified by what God has actually declared to be, or it is not. A belief cannot be justified or true if it is outside of or contrary to what God has declared. A belief is neither wise nor prudent if it disagrees with God's expressed word.

Our desire may well be to not believe in Hell at all. But the Scriptures do not give us that option. Hell is a revealed truth that we must confess if we are to be faithful to God and His revelation. Our desire may even be to lessen its severity, but we cannot go beyond what our all-wise, all-good, and all-just God has said that it is. He revealed its reality, and He told us that it is indeed a fearful reality. Our desire is rightly for none to go to that place or state, but we must be truthful about it if we are to make up a hedge and warn men to flee from that coming wrath.

What is Hell? Every time we find the word "hell" translated into English, it is not necessarily speaking of final judgment. Hell, as it relates to our topic, is that which pertains to the final judgment yet to come upon man. The term "hell" has other general uses. Sometimes it simply means the place (*sheol*) of the dead or where the dead go (Ps 16:10). Jesus at one point used the term "hell" metaphorically to describe the power of death, and thus of the devil, when He said that the gates of hell (*hadés*) would not prevail against His church (Matt 16:18). The term "hell" could be broader than that. It could mean a place of peace where the righteous would go or a place of torment where the wicked would go (Ps 9:17 compared with Ps 16:10). Sometimes the word "hell" was used in the Old Testament for the grave itself (Gen 42:38). That does not insinuate that the Old Testament writers rejected a belief in life after, or rather beyond, physical death. They uniformly did believe in life beyond death, as we shall deal with in the proceeding study. They further taught, whether spatially in terms of a differing view of cosmology or in terms of modern physics of interdimensional realities, that hell was downward (Ps 55:15), a special theme adopted by New Testament writers regarding heaven being upward (II Cor 12:2).

Ultimately, the prevailing view of the Old Testament, especially second temple Judaism as portrayed in the days of Christ, portrayed a view that 'hell' is a place, synonymous with the grave, where the dead would go until judgment; the righteous to wait in felicity and the wicked to wait in torment. That was the understanding of "hell" as illuminated by Christ in the story of Lazarus and the rich man (Luke 16:19–31). In that story, "hell" was the name given to the place of torment that the rich man entered into after death and Paradise was the place that Lazarus entered. They were, spatially or dimensionally speaking, residing congruent to one another, and only separated by something called a great gulf. They were able to see one another, but unable to cross the demarcation.

But this use of the term hell is not the final judgment. Essentially, at that point, hell and Paradise were in the same place. Christ, at His death, told the thief that trusted in Him that they would be together in Paradise, which answered to the term "hell" in prophecy (I Pet 3:19, Ps 16:10). When the Apostles' Creed says that Christ descended into hell, that is what is meant.

It is not that that the above view of hell is wrong but that it changed in the light of what Christ accomplished in His death and resurrection. It was foretold that Christ would lead captivity captive (Eph 4:8), and after the resurrection of Christ, Paul spoke of Paradise, either spatially or dimensionally, as upward in a distinctly different place (II Cor 12:2–5). The way into the holiest place, the throne of God, was finally made by Christ and now when the believer is absent from this body they are present with the Lord (II Cor 5:10, Heb 9:8). Therefore, by the time we reach the end of the canon, "hell" came to be understood as the place where the wicked would go at physical death while they await their resurrection and final judgment (Rev. 20:11–15).

The time will come when death and "hell" shall be cast into the lake of fire, which is the final judgment. This final judgment is the everlasting contempt that was anticipated by Daniel that we will shortly see. This meaning is what we declare to be the Hell of final judgment.

Often, when Christ spoke of Hell He did not use terms like *sheol* or *hades*, which were the words often translated in English as 'hell' in the Old and New Testaments. *Sheol* and *hades* were words used to speak of the grave or of the temporary place of the dead. Instead, the word *gehenna* was frequently used by Christ and was also traditionally translated using the word "hell." This word is related to the Old Testament word *Thophet*. This is the Hell of final judgment. The grave, or where the dead go at death, is temporary. Christ taught of a place that would be permanent.

The imagery of Hell in this sense is one of fire. In the days of the kings of Judah, the valley of the sons of Hinnom was a place outside the gates of Jerusalem where hideous human sacrifices of live human beings, often children and babies, were cast into the fire of an idol (II Chr. 28:3, 33:6, Jer. 7:31, 32:35). Even when that practice ended centuries later in the days of Christ, that valley was the place where the trash was continually burned. It was a tangible reality to all who heard Christ speak. It was something they could see, hear, and smell as they passed by the continuous fire. It was this use of the word 'hell' that informed and gave full substance to the doctrine of Hell as taught by Christ. It describes and gives imagery a reality that is final in its execution, irredeemable in its effect.

The doctrine of Hell is the theological heritage of the eschatology of Christ Himself. It bears the authority of the One who rose from the grave and has all authority. The eschatology of Christ is that there will be a resurrection of the dead and that resurrection will be of the just and the unjust. There will be a resurrection to life and a resurrection to damnation (John 5:28, 29). It is the latter that is the subject here. Christ Himself will be the judge of all who are raised on that last day.

In His parables, Christ described the reality of the resurrection of damnation. By use of analogy, from the parable to its interpretation, He concluded that it is where the wicked will be cast into the furnace of fire, and where there will be weeping and gnashing of teeth (Matt 13:42, 50). Christ intended for these truths to structure our understanding of the eschatology of man. Each man will experience one of two possible ends or finalities. He told us to fear the One that is able to cast both body and soul in Hell (Matt 10:28). The doctrine of Hell naturally follows the biblical truth that after this present life there will be judgment (Heb 9:27).

It is no valid contradiction or argument against Hell to say that Old Covenant documents have no clear teaching concerning it. Such an argument is both untrue and ineffective, even if it was found true. The doctrine of Christ mirrors the words of Daniel (which will be highlighted shortly), but it does not stand or fall on that truth or whether there is Old Testament support elsewhere. Christ said He was expounding matters hidden since the foundation of the world, and that His parables included the doctrine of Hell and final judgment (Matt 13:35). The doctrine of Hell is distinctly Christian. It is not contradictory to say that Christ offered clear teaching on that which was not fully known before. There are many things that are more fully revealed in the New Covenant by Christ and those taught by Him. What Christ and His apostles taught about Hell is authoritative, even if there is a seeming absence of support anywhere else on the matter. Unless there is a clear contradiction between the Old Testament writers on this matter, then the teaching of Christ and those that followed in His doctrine is not overturned by the seeming silence of Moses and the prophets.

Obviously, there is no clear reason for Moses and the writers of the books of history to teach about the afterlife. Christ did teach that their writings were sufficient to warn men so they might not end up in a place of torment (Luke 16:27–31). But it must be understood that their moral and salvific doctrines were sufficient to turn men from that end (II Tim 3:15–17). The concern of Moses and the writers of history were to teach covenantal history and to teach law. These writers definitely showed a belief in resurrection, despite claims to the contrary. They demonstrated it by:

- Their burial of the dead, showing their hope of resurrection (Gen 23:19);
- The present tense Lordship of God to those who passed on (as later expounded by Christ, Matt 22:32);
- The description of death as being a departure (Gen. 35:1), and the departure of Enoch and Elijah (Gen 5:24, II Kings 2:11);
- Job, which is the oldest written book in the Bible, taught about the afterlife (Job 19:26);
- David and Solomon also both taught about the afterlife and resurrection (Ps 16:10, Ecc 12:7);
- Isaiah followed suit (Isa 26:19);
- The Old Testament writers did not blush to use terms like forever when discussing their hope in God (Ps 23:6).

More could be expounded on ideas like Abraham being promised by God to inherit a land with his seed, which he did not do in this life, or David and his seed having an everlasting kingdom. Covenants like this demand the afterlife. And it is worth mentioning that the effect of second temple Judaism is a populace that believed Elijah and the prophets could and would return.

Daniel foreshadowed and mirrored the teaching of Christ on the subject of Hell. He posited two possibilities for future existence. Some will awake to everlasting life (Dan 12:2). Some will close their eyes in this life and be raised to a reality of perpetual life; that is a life of felicity, life invigorating and enlivening. It is life because it is connected to a full fellowship with God who is the source of all life. However, Daniel spoke of another everlasting state. This state was not something that he could call life, but he rather called it shame and everlasting contempt (Dan 12:2). That is the fearful fate Christ spoke of. It is not called life, but it reflects consciousness with words like shame and contempt. Therefore, by the loss of the word *life*, it does not mean non-living. It is balanced as everlasting, just like life, and therefore intends either the same durative or qualitative nature of that blessed state. One may safely infer equal duration or endlessness to both the blessedness and cursed ends as both are modified by the term eternal or everlasting (*olam*). At least, whatever the sense we give that modifier in its connection with life, we must do also with the state of cursing. More on this shortly, when we speak of the parallels in the declaration of Christ.

There is the qualitative sense of continuing with concepts of shame and contempt intended by Daniel. We may simply call this a sense of awareness. It is not called life simply because of its separation from the source of life, God. John called this place death, or rather, the second death (Rev. 21:8). Those who enter therein are called the dead; dead to God, dead in sins; but here they are aware, conscious, and connected in a corporeal way to that world in which they will exist. Existing, but not living or thriving, they consciously know only a sense of shame and a reality of contempt.

According to Daniel, many will be raised from the dust of death and will meet this fate, as will many also who go into life. It does not intend to say that some will not go into either end. All are subsumed by both of the ends considered. Many or a multitude will come to judgment and receive it as such, and many would be received into life. An alternative interpretation will be dealt with shortly, but suffice it to say for now that Daniel declared these as the two possible fates.

When Christ spoke of being condemned already, this shame and everlasting contempt was the fate He was referencing. The doctrine of Hell, this cannot be repeated enough, is meant to be a fearful doctrine (Matt 10:28). It is a place for both body and soul, which speaks of resurrection. It is destruction (Matt 7:13). God destroys body and soul there. Whether there is an intent of Christ to speak of an eventual end to mortality is not a necessary conclusion of the word destroy (*apollumi*). This destruction (*olethros*) is eternal in nature (II Thess 1:9). The idea is the ruin of a thing primarily, and not its extinction. It is called destruction because it is complete and final in its execution, and in the spirit of Daniel it is everlasting because it will be suspended in its reality without hope of reform or reconstruction. Like Sodom or Tyre, its destruction is permanent. The body and soul will be brought to its end in the sense that it will be brought to its inevitable conclusion where it will remain without any further process. Like wood is reduced to ash in its destruction, so will the body and soul be of those that are brought into that place of destruction. The wood still exists and has its being, but it is ash and now irreducible. Thus, men ought to fear. What happens in that reality to come is complete and final; a state that cannot be reduced or humbled any lower than it is. A state that cannot hope to be reformed. A ruined or destroyed city can no longer offer any comfort or protection.

Christ continued to give definition to this irreducible state of the damned. Christ described Hell as the place where "their worm" dies not and where the fire is not quenched (Mark 9:43–48). Christ drew from the language of Isaiah (Isa 66:24) to describe the fearfulness of this final judgment. He repeatedly declared that in that place or that state there shall be weeping and gnashing of teeth. Christ also in that text beseeched all to avoid it at all costs, to take extreme steps, if need be, to not come to that end. These words give a body to Christ's doctrine. The final eternal home of the damned is a state of *consciousness, endlessness,* and *torment.*

As an irreducible state, Hell is the place where those who are finally damned are reduced to something like a worm. This is its *consciousness.* The possessive personal pronoun "their" speaks of the essential person. The essential person will still be there, possessing something. That sense of possessing will include the possession of faculties like intelligence, volition, and sensibilities. The term *worm* is what those faculties that are yet possessed have been reduced to. It is the lowest common denominator of the nature of humanity. The personal pronoun speaks of the sustained humanity or personhood, and the worm speaks of the reduced state. Those now spiritually dead will be the spiritually destroyed.

Whether the term *worm* is meant to speak of the reduced state of the body, or the reduced state of the soul, is not clear. The term worm in the Scriptures first speaks of a state of decay (Ex 16:20, Deut 29:18, Job 7:5, 17:14, 19:26, 21:26, 24:20). It may speak of the eternal decay of the body; a state connected with bodily suffering like Job's experience, who longed to die but could not. In this sense, the phrase "their worm dies not" would mean corruption of the body, suspended in the state of decay, decayed but not consumed. The rich man in hell was described by Christ as having all his bodily senses. He had ears by which he heard the rebuke of Abraham, eyes that he could see his torment and the missed state of Paradise, a tongue that he could taste and feel the scorched state of fiery torment, and a sense of touch that caused him to cry out that he was tormented in the flames. The rich man sought bodily comfort for relief and could find none (Luke 16:19–31). Hell, like heaven, will not be absent of bodily senses and thus is connected with a resurrection.

Another sense of the word *worm* is the humility of the person themselves, the soul of men (Ps 22:6). This answers to the shame that Daniel described (Dan 12:2). The first will forever be made the last with no possibility of restoration. These will forever be humbled in the sense that they will be suspended in that humbled state. Both of these ideas could be inferred by the text, fully self-aware as to their bodily senses and as to their own humbled spiritual state.

So also, Christ described the *endlessness* of their state. Their worm dies not and the fire is not quenched. Christ presents these descriptions to us, not in any allegorical sense, but as blank statements of fact. The emphasis on the endless nature is even greater than that of the conscious nature. The statement is that their worm "shall not die" and the fire "will not be extinguished." Like the bush that burned with the presence of God in the days of Moses, this fire burns, but does not consume (Ex 3:2). It does not say that it cannot be quenched, as if this is a statement of something that is beyond the almighty power of God, but rather that it "is not quenched." God shall not extinguish this fire. Christ believed and taught that Hell would not be brought to an end.

While we cannot understand the intersection of the eternality of God and the temporality of our existence and how those two concepts of duration can intersect, Christ described Hell as damnation (Matt 23:22) and called the finality of Hell eternal damnation (Mark 3:29). There is something of the eternal nature of God that sustains Hell, just as it will sustain the state of the blessed. It is described as fire, for our God is a consuming fire, and it is a fearful thing to fall into the hands of the living God (Heb 10:29, 31). To enter into Hell is to enter into the fearful and eternal presence of the eternal wrath of an eternal God. It is to know God only in His wrath forever.

When we die physically, we return to God (Ecc 12:7). Those who are saved return to Him in the state of His grace and eternal felicity; they are eternally in the presence of His love. Those who are lost return unto God in the sense of His wrath, separated from love, grace, and mercy forever. Hell is hidden in the eternal nature of God. It is fire indeed. Fire is something that we can relate to in this life. It burns and sears in great intensity and torment. Hell is everlasting fire and everlasting destruction (Matt 18:8, 19:29, 25:41, 46). To be everlasting is to be never ending, and thus it is unquenchable in its nature. It will never reach its vanishing point. That is the terror of the term "is not quenched" as proclaimed by Christ. There will be no relief. There will be no comfort. There will be no drop of water to cool the tongue of those who are tormented in those flames. The temporal life of the damned will be suspended in an open-ended future in the eternal existence of the wrath of God.

Moving forward, Hell is also a state of *torment*. Christ echoes that which was already seen in Daniel. Christ described the experience of Hell as "weeping and gnashing of teeth." There is a definite correlation between the description of Christ and the description of Daniel who spoke of "shame and everlasting contempt." The description of Christ however speaks of both mental and physical anguish, whereas Daniel fixed only on the former. The weeping speaks of the emptiness of joy, which is the opposite of heaven that is called the joy of our Lord (Matt 25:21). Hell will be a place of sorrow; a continuing present sorrow, as the tense of the verb weeping intends. The concept that Hell is a place for the rebels of this life to revel in their rebellion for all eternity, a great party if you will, is a falsity. Foolish pictures of poetry gave rise to this point of view, like the devil of Milton who said that he would rather reign in hell than serve in heaven. Generations of people have rebelled against God in their lives believing that Hell will be a heaven for them where they will have endless fellowship and reveling. Christ said to the contrary that there will be weeping.

This anguish answers to the dual nature of humanity; spiritual and physical. As there will be weeping for the sorrow of the soul so there will be gnashing of teeth to express the pain of the body. This is the resurrection of damnation, a literal bodily existence after the pattern of Christ, but only to shame and not to glory. Hell is a physical reality. Gnashing speaks of intense grinding, as one would do when bearing a great pain or great rage. It is the physical expression of great turmoil. If we take it to speak of the bearing of great pain, the unbearable suffering is being highlighted. "The wicked shall see it and be grieved; he shall gnash with his teeth, and melt away: the desire of the wicked shall perish." (Ps 112:10) However, the term often takes on the meaning of rage and intense hatred. "All thine enemies have opened their mouth against thee: they hiss and gnash the teeth. . . ." (Lam 2:16)

Hell, then, will be a place reduced to the greatest discord, unlike the harmony of heaven. As the Pharisees gnashed upon Stephen with their teeth in their hatred, so will the reality of Hell be the enduring feeling of intense hatred. As they remain in their sinful condition and in enmity against God, they will be filled with intense and endless hatred and rage against anything that bears whatever image of God that still remains (in them or in others). There will be no fellowship in Hell, but an intense hatred for others and an intense feeling of being hated by others. There will be a great and lonely self-centeredness in hell, an absence of love and empathy. Man will be alone in pain and self-loathing, drawing no comfort from anything around them.

The torment of Hell also comes from its prevailing imagery, fire. The rich man said he was tormented in the flame (Luke 16:24). There is no image more hideous than the picture of one burning in flames. The thought of burning even a portion of oneself brings to mind intense pain, but to be engulfed in flames is unthinkable. When one is on fire, they seek death; they cry, they convulse, they scream. To be suspended in that moment is definitely the reality that Christ wanted to convey to the sinner. Following the direct teaching of John the Baptist (Mark 4:10, 12), Christ in fifteen distinct references referred to Hell as fire (Matt. 5:22, 7:19, 13:40, 42, 50, 18:8, 9, 25:41, Mark 9:43, 44, 45, 46, 47, 48, 49).

It may be said that fire is simply a metaphor for the wrath of God. If it were intended to be a metaphor, then that would give no reason for any to believe that the suffering of Hell is something less intense or less real. In those times where Christ spoke of fire, He used indicative verbs relating the fire to reality (Matt 5:22, 13:42, etc.). Hell is, after all, a real physical place for those physically resurrected. When one denies that Hell is fire, it usually indicates that they hold a metaphorically interpreted reality of Hell; a belief that operates outside of the indicative language of the Scriptures. But whatever may be said of Hell as a Scripturally revealed truth, Christ used the language of reality to describe its torment.

Another image invoked of Hell is darkness. Three times in the book of Matthew Christ is recorded as referring to Hell as outer darkness (Matt 8:12, 22:13, 25:30). Two of these are in parable form, but the first (Matt 8:12) shares the same indicative reality as the imagery of fire. God is light in the sense that He reveals Himself. Hell as darkness will be the end of revelation, which could have been a source of comfort. Nothing new will be said to the wicked, for the conviction of final judgment is just that, final. There will be no new epoch to come for them. It is darkness, according to Christ, that men loved instead of light because their deeds were evil (John 3:19). It was a plague upon the Egyptians, a darkness that can be felt (Ex 10:2) and is mirrored by the plague of darkness in the Apocalypse where men will gnaw their tongues for pain (Rev 16:10). Outer darkness seems to be metaphoric language for separation from the benefits of Christ's rule, and to be outside the light of the glory of His grace.

There is also definite physical and mental suffering connected with darkness. We naturally fear the dark. To be left in darkness for long will cause panic in the strongest of men. Sulfur burns with a dark flame, and Hell elsewhere is described as fire and brimstone (Rev 21:8). Darkness and fire are not contradictory images of that state. Peter would later declare that this mist of darkness is everlasting (II Pet. 2:7). The angst of darkness will not end. There will be no comfort or expectation of light in any sense of its meaning.

Two more words are indicative of the reality of the torment of Hell, condemnation and damnation. Salvation is from condemnation (John 5:24). Hell *is* that condemnation; the righteous judgment upon the guilty. The entire world shall become guilty before God (Rom 3:19, 20). The books will be opened, and men shall be rightly condemned according to their works. There will not be a single person in Hell that will not know themselves to be guilty and deserving of that end.

Then Christ also used the word damnation. For some there is a greater damnation. Christ asked the hypocrites how they should escape the damnation of hell (Matt 23:14, 23). Those that blaspheme the Holy Spirit are in danger of eternal damnation (Mark 3:29). The fate of the lost was summed up by Christ saying, "They that have done evil, unto the resurrection of damnation." (John 5:29) To be damned is akin to the term condemnation. It is the final and irrevocable decision to punish the wrongdoer. It is final. There will be no place of repentance there. Thus, when Christ says, "depart from me" to the workers of iniquity, those will be the most horrible words they will ever hear; the last words of revelation they will ever hear (Matt 7:23). To depart from Christ is to finally depart from salvation and the embodiment and presence of the love of God. It will be to enter into Hell that was created for the devil and his angels. It will be to take one's part and lot among evil and its consequences forever. It will, in the sense of the word damnation, take on the fulness of God's curse. It will be a world without end.

The apostles that were sent out by Christ echoed the same message as to the consciousness, endlessness, and torment of Hell. Matthew, Mark, Luke, and John are distinct witnesses as to what the apostles taught, providing a summary of Christ's earthly ministry. Most of what we are told about Hell and the nature of the final judgment is found therein. What the apostles said is what Christ taught about Hell and should be decisive for any Christian debate since all authority belongs to Christ. They also showed what John the Baptist taught about Hell, as the last of the Old Covenant prophets (Matt 3:10). Hell is then the infallible capstone of Old and New Testament doctrine revealed and interpreted.

Setting aside the four Gospels, the rest of the New Testament writings march in perfect harmony with what Christ taught. Paul described the state of the lost as "indignation and wrath, tribulation and anguish. . . ." (Rom 2:7–9) Paul went on to teach that those that are lost "shall be punished with everlasting destruction from the presence of the Lord and from the glory of his power. . ." (II Thess 1:9). The writer of Hebrews called it "fiery indignation, which shall devour the adversaries. . . ." (Heb 10:27) Peter called it the fire and perdition reserved for the ungodly (II Pet 3:7). Jude said it was the vengeance of eternal fire, reserved blackness of darkness forever (Jude 1:7, 13). John clearly taught in the Revelation that Hell was a lake of fire, where those who inhabit it are tormented forever and ever (Rev 14:11, 20:11–15).

This makes up the faith that was delivered to the saints regarding final judgment. There is room here for some level of disagreement as to the meaning of some of the terms. There is, however, no room for ignoring these words and what they clearly mean. Again, it cannot be stated that there is no Hell. Christ does not leave that option open. It cannot be dismissed as a metaphor. Like all aspects of our faith, it must be received as God has declared it. Everything that we think, feel, believe, and do is and ought to be subject to the correction of the Scriptures (John 17:17). To accept Hell as it is taught is to accept it as a fearful doctrine, a trembling reality declared to be so by the only true God.

With that being said, we must ask ourselves if it is possible to hold to the fearfulness intended by the doctrine without holding to its endlessness conscious torment. There are brethren that hold to annihilation or conditional mortality (a belief that the sufferings of hell will come to an end with the eventual extinguishment of the person). While some teach this in earnestness, not intending to diminish its fearfulness (its conscious torment), others hold to these doctrines to avoid its fearfulness against philosophical and emotional objections (See the next chapter on Lordship). Attempts to temper that fearfulness are to be rebuked by the Scripture. But what shall we say of those who wish to uphold the Scriptures and hold that Hell will have an end; an end to torment and conscious existence? We approach this question with clarity and brotherly kindness. Whatever our doctrine of Hell is, it must agree with the Scriptures. It must be a reality to be fled and escaped from. It is a trembling reality.

What matters in the end is that our belief is text-driven, for that alone honors the truth that God has spoken. That is what has been attempted thus far in this treatise, prayerfully by the grace of God. Admittedly, broad theories of theology can possibly be true, but that matters little if the theory cannot explain the data found in the text. For instance, the conditionalist may be right in saying that a belief in the immortal (e.g., eternal) soul is not a scriptural truth, but something drawn out of pagan and Platonic philosophy. One can admit that there is a great amount of truth in this point. God alone is eternal, Christ alone has life in Himself. He alone has immortality and dwells in the light that no man can approach. All of us have only contingent life (I Tim 1:17, 6:16). I would not argue to the contrary on a philosophical or even on a biblical level.

Any arguments that attempt to meet the conditionalist at this level of theology are foolhardy. For instance, if one might say life is the breath of God and God's breath cannot be destroyed, that one would run afoul of the text, for death is breathing the last breath and God withdrawing His breath from creatures. Conditionalists are just as capable as we who call ourselves traditionalists in making valid Scriptural observations.

Another instance of a true conditionalist claim is that mankind in the garden had conditional mortality (in this physical world at least) and needed to eat from the Tree of Life in order to continue to live or rather live forever (Gen 3:22). And it is true that it is those in heaven that have a right to the tree of life (Rev 22:14). The nature of death will be given fuller treatment in a later chapter, as well the nature of such Gospel realities, and will only devolve here into unneeded contention. The contention of conditionalism here stands as true at its face value for now. Mankind was created with conditional life.

However, this does not establish conditionalism as a valid approach to our belief in Hell. The simple question to ask the conditionalist regarding mortality and immortality is this; if you believe rightly that the life of the damned is conditional, as is those in heaven, does this say anything to negate God upholding their everlasting existence as He will with those in heaven? Simply proving the conditional existence of us as creatures does not touch on or explain the meaning of any text that proclaims final judgment. What will be done with the text and its assertions? This is the challenge of their position. The problem with conditionalism is the text, and despite mounting some valid arguments regarding some specific texts, they find themselves in an endless loop of talking around specific texts and their natural meaning.

Consider one example with a conditional exegesis of Daniel 12. It may be true that there was no uniform understanding that Daniel taught on the resurrection prior to the advent of Christ. The words of Daniel are thus:

> "And at that time thy people shall be delivered, every one that shall be found written in the book. And many of them that sleep in the dust of the earth shall awake, some to everlasting life, and some to shame and everlasting contempt. And they that be wise shall shine as the brightness of the firmament; and they that turn many to righteousness as the stars for ever and ever." Daniel 12:1, 2

It is not an invalid use of the text, as conditionalism maintains, to say that this text is about those who were faithful in the persecution prophesied in Daniel's eleventh chapter, as recorded historically in the Maccabees. At least, it is indicative of a pre-Christ understanding of many. These faithful were the elect of God who would be lifted up in everlasting remembrance, shining as lights, great signs, or examples for future generations. Those who were not faithful would be held in contempt by future generations. Many secular theologians and philosophers hold that same view today; that we will all live on in the pages of history famously or infamously. With this interpretation, the conditionalist seems to have a compelling argument isolating this text.

However, it is obvious that Christ did not hold such a meaning of resurrection and offered the understood meaning of Daniel commonly held today. If Christ interpreted the meaning of resurrection, then that is its true or ultimate meaning.

> "[Christ said] The hour is coming, in the which all that are in the graves shall hear his voice, and shall come forth; they that have done good, unto the resurrection of life; and they that have done evil, unto the resurrection of damnation." John 5:28, 29

Daniel is not disconnected from Christ, and its true interpretation is founded by Christ. Let us not renew the Pharisee versus Sadducee historical-grammatical debate as if Christ did not speak and give meaning to Daniel. Again, Christ said, "these shall go away into everlasting punishment: but the righteous into life eternal." The language of Daniel in both cases is invoked by Christ (Matt 25:46). To read Daniel as if we were Sadducees denying the reality of the resurrection is dishonoring to what Christ our Head has revealed. One can talk around Daniel only at the cost of distorting what Christ clearly taught about resurrection using Daniel's language. Even if the flat historical-grammatical interpretation holds some interpretive value in the immediate context, we are bound to give our ears to the authority of Christ here. We cannot clearly hold that we shall *forever* be with the Lord in our heavenly hope declared by Christ in such a limited exegesis. We interpret the Old Testament in the light of the New Testament. Further, there is nothing in the context to demand an interpretation of "shame and contempt" as a reality only for those of us that are reading their history instead of a reality for the actual unnamed actors of the righteous and sinful deeds. The later idea fits the whole of revelation and not the former.

There are further seemingly valid semantic arguments for conditionalism. Fire has a destroying purpose. Other purposes for fire are also legitimate such as for a sign (like the burning bush), for purifying (such as removing dross from gold), or a memorial (such as the continual fire on the altar). However, since the fire of Hell is connected to its destructive purpose, the semantics of destruction is a powerful argument put forth by the conditionalist. Fire will devour the adversaries of the Lord (Heb 10:27, though this text is possibly not about the final judgment, Matt 22:7). Hell will destroy the body and soul of those subject to it (Matt 10:28, *apollumi*,— II Thess 1:9, *olethros*). For one to contend that the nature of destruction means that something comes to an end is not an invalid use of semantics. After all, Herod was moved to destroy the babies in Matthew 2, and the babies ceased to exist in this world. It does not, however, negate the opposite understanding of something being reduced to rubble or brought to its end (i.e., final state), as formerly argued above. The punishment of eternal destruction is, after all, described as something related to being sent "from the presence" of the coming Lord, and not something ceasing to be (II Thess 1:9). This relates to the direct teaching of Christ regarding final judgment (Matt 7:21–23). To hold otherwise is to deny the reality of Hell in total, for if destruction is a thing coming to an end then there is no conscious suffering either. All would end at that moment of judgment. In their zeal to deny endlessness, conscious torment (i.e., the fearfulness of Hell) is denied too.

Conditionalist semantics does not dismiss traditional arguments to the contrary. What it does is contend with the clear reading of other texts that say the result of the destruction of this fire is that ". . . the smoke of their torment ascends up for ever and ever: and they have no rest day nor night. . . ." (Rev 14:10, 11) It is conscious torment that belongs to them, and its smoke goes up from age to age, without end. If the conditionalist argues that it is the smoke that remains as a memorial, then they are left to explain the absence of "rest day and night." The only argument left then is to appeal to the apocalyptic language of the Revelation which comes close to dismissing the possibility of any meaning being drawn from that book. We add similar concerns with a similar text, "[the dragon will be cast] where the beast and the false prophet are, and shall be tormented day and night for ever and ever." (Rev 20:10) The enemies of our Lord are described as subject to continuous torment. The semantical contortions necessary to escape the plain meaning of the text are too great to maintain.

The tenure of all this is that, while making legitimate points at times about context and semantics, the conditionalist must continually sidestep what appears to be the clear and natural reading of many texts. The undying worm and unquenchable fire described by Christ, as the fearful end from which the wise will go to extreme measures to escape, must be dismissed as not perfectly congruent with the imagery of the same wording invoked from Isaiah (Isa 66:24). Christ cannot, according to the conditionalist, have any other meaning other than what was in Isaiah's immediate context. And Christ must not be speaking of duration when he compares everlasting punishment with everlasting life, but rather (as a conditionalist would argue) punishment that belongs to the ages to come and life that belongs to those same ages (Matt 25:46). The text can never, in their eyes, intuitively mean what it appears to mean or how Christ and the apostles appear to be using it.

The conditionalist view may never be fully defeated by the traditional view presented in the earlier arguments of this chapter. This is because some clever interpretation can be brought forth that seems to explain away a particular text, but those explanations never fully explain the other sets of biblical data. The detractor ends up chasing their tail and never coming to an actual firm doctrine. Hell as a doctrine, though, is a revealed doctrine. It is God at His Word that must be believed. Sinners as sinners will have their end. It will be an end that includes conscious torment. And it is presented to us by God as an endless end or reality. We may engage in striving with the revealed truth found in the text, but in the final analysis it says what it says. The sinner will one day receive from God the fruit of their own way, will go to a place of their own, fitting to their nature, and so it shall ever be. Flee, not from the prospect of annihilation and nothingness, but from the wrath to come (Matt 3:7, Luke 3:7).

Chapter 4

Hell Is the Exercise of the Sovereign Will of the Lord Over His Creatures

"Hath not the potter power over the clay, of the same lump to make one vessel unto honor, and another unto dishonor?"

ROMANS 9:21

THE SUBJECT OF HELL is too often approached as if God was on trial and must sit in the dock and answer man's charges against Him. The cliche that all who are in prison are innocent is the mindset analogous to this view. The doctrine of Hell, however, is the clear declaration that the opposite is true. There is a just Lawgiver who has given just laws to men, and they have transgressed them. They stand before Him now as the Perfect Judge of their crimes and He will judge them righteously in accordance with His Law. There is a theme that runs through the Scripture that encapsulates what the penalty against sin is. Your sin will result in death. The death penalty has hung over mankind from the beginning. Man knew that the day he ate the fruit it meant death (Gen 2:17). God stated that the soul that sins shall die (Ezek 18:4). It is this judgment of death that answers the true nature of Hell and its justice. More about the just penalty of death in the following chapter.

The vile repudiation of God against the idea of Hell is the cry of a guilty conscience that will not admit to its guilt or its need of repentance. They will not in their rebellion have God rule over them. They will not let go of their sin but instead declare themselves righteous in their own eyes. They reject any sense of a need for mercy and grace. And, therefore, they vilely mock the idea that they must be judged and the reality of Hell that represents that fearful judgment. They hate the idea that their choices have real and eternal consequences. They hate the idea that they deserve such a fate.

To our contemporaries, the idea of Hell represents all that is wrong or toxic with Christianity. They say that it is contrary to the idea that God is love. "A God of love would not punish a person for all eternity in a lake of fire," is the general refrain. Thus, Hell becomes a theological hurdle to nominal Christianity, one that must be rubbed out of our doctrinal statements. They say, rather, we must hold to a God of love and reject the sadistic picture of God malevolently roasting the wicked on spits over the fire (an imagery no biblically faithful mind would affirm). In their minds, Hell must be abandoned to make Christianity a palatable and respectable faith contextualized with the larger non-judgmental culture.

The nominal Christian world is not the only one who takes issue with the idea of Hell. The secular world has the same issues. The average person will believe in Hell only for the most evil of mankind or for the person that just dared to offend them but never for themselves or those close to them. Stalin, Hitler, and Dahmer surely will be there but hardly no one else. They imagine themselves to be pretty good people and believe that God will have to allow them into heaven because of how good they are. The intellectual person will dismiss Hell as a concept altogether. They proclaim the ideas of God, morality, the existence of an immaterial soul, free will, and justice have no actual reality. They hide behind a worldview of materialism and naturalism, declaring that only the material world exists and the laws of nature that govern, while ignoring the huge moral and metaphysical absurdities such a view of the world entails. Hell, for them, is part of the ignorant myths that unenlightened humanity once held to.

Hell is reduced to a punch line levied against the knuckle-dragging Christians that still walk in unenlightened ignorance. Hell is also reduced only to a literary or allegorical figure of some other thing. The mystic or existentialist might say that Hell is the realm of our current experience. Sartre famously quipped that Hell was other people. Mirroring eastern metaphysical philosophies, the mystic may assert that the physical world is either evil or an evil allusion, likening it to Hell. Hell is this illusion of life, and one may escape Hell (since it is not eternal) through the works-based salvation of self-discipline by detaching from this physical world and all the things in it.

These fanciful ideologies have all cast off the reality of justice in their attempt to shield themselves from negative consequences of a judgment that possesses finality. However, we live in a real world, and what happens here is meaningful. Every act we do is in a moral context subject to real and final sanction. Justice will be meted out in the life to come. And if not there, where? If not there, it is found nowhere. In such a scheme, there is no justice and no meaning. But we are headed to our long home (Ecc 12:5), our everlasting house, and there we will meet our God. I plead now with the reader, prepare to meet your God.

I repeat, if justice is only in the here and now, then justice is not real, for we do not see it in this world. Its concept is only a cruel joke played on insignificant humanity. There is no greater existential reality proclaimed than that we are free to choose our actions, and we are accountable for the same. No such accounting happens here in this world except in the rarest of circumstances and only with a limited scope. However, there will be an accounting. We know in our hearts the abiding truth, "after this the judgment." (Heb 9:27) That judgment to the guilty is death. No one has to convince us of this, our conscience cries out that it is true, and we fear it and physical death because of it.

There can be no Christian arguments against the concept of Hell, for such would abandon the truth of revelation. To deny the reality of Hell one must turn to secular arguments drawn from the supposed Problem of Evil. Such arguments attempt to displace God as the ultimate Judge who we all must face. The aim of the Problem of Evil argument as it applies to Hell is to deny Hell by denying the existence of God, or by denying the justice of God, or by denying the mercy or love of God. In other words, if Hell exists (the argument goes), then God is either unjust or unloving. Therefore, such a God cannot exist. Hell is presented as evidence that the God of the Scriptures is not real. And it leaves room ultimately for a new god to be formed that does not need to be feared, for it does not judge, or a new a eschatology where all are safe.

The Problem of Evil argument in any of its forms begins with the assumption that mankind can sit in judgment over the Lord of all and over the truths He has revealed. The traditional form of the argument is as such:

- If God is all-powerful, He could end suffering or evil.

- If God is all-good, He would not allow suffering or evil to exist.
- Christians proclaim that God is both all-powerful and all-good.
- Evil or suffering exist.
- Therefore, the Christian God is either not all-powerful or is not all-good.
- Therefore, the Christian God does not exist.

There are several problems with this logic, chiefly that it presents a false and dishonest dilemma. It hand-picks only the revealed truths of God that the arguer wishes to use, leaving out those that are inconvenient to the argument. God is far more than just all-good and all-power in His perfections. For instance, God is also all-wise. If evil and suffering exist, then an all-wise God would have a reason to permit it or even cause it without contradicting His power and goodness (for a fuller treatment of the Problem of Evil generally, see Appendix).

Worst yet, the arguer claims to be all-knowing, in that they declare that God can have no just cause for the present reality (e.g., judgment of sin, etc.). The point here is this; no human being with their limited knowledge is able to sit in judgment of God. We do not have the knowledge, power, or righteousness to be His judge.

When applied to Hell, the bent of the Problem of Evil argument is ultimately the same, the attempt to say that there is no God above us, at least one we should fear. It sets up man not only as the judge of God, but also believing that they have displaced God as their own god. In displacing God they have rather been forced to embrace nihilism. They are left with a world without truth, goodness, and beauty; without purpose, intelligence, sensibility, morality, and volition. Reality is random, indiscernible, impersonal, and unknowable; for there is no ground to believe that it can be anything else. They cannot, in their suppression of the truth of God, affirm anything about the world around them. It defies reason to deny the existence of God in order to escape the symbol of ultimate justice, which Hell represents.

The rebellious naturally bring their secular arguments to bear in the denial of Hell, the ultimate form of suffering. The problem of Evil argument needs only be morphed slightly to accommodate their rebellion. It is now argued that if Hell exists, then either God is not just or God does not love. Armed with the irrationality of their secular Problem of Evil approach, they feel like they have cleverly done away with the God of revelation in general and the fear of Hell in specific. Yet, the argument offers a false set of choices in its rebellion just as it does in its other uses. The Scriptures demonstrate clearly that Hell does not deny the justice or the love of God and, therefore, fells the folly of fools. The rebellious vainly attempts to avoid final judgment.

If one chooses to claim that the God of the Scriptures does not exist, there would be no epistemological basis for believing or affirming anything including the reality of justice or love. Since the revealed God of truth is indeed there, justice is a reality and Hell as its ultimate symbol is not in contradiction to justice. The idea that God is not just if He sends people to Hell borders on insanity. It is tantamount to saying that it would be unjust for God to exercise His perfect justice.

Further, if there is no merited judgment after this life, then morality does not now exist. There is no reason not to be a Hitler, or a Dahmer, or a Jack the Ripper, especially if you believed you could get away with it or experience no negative present consequences for it. The denying of God's justice is basically an argument that maintains that man should be free from all judgment and able to do whatever they want to do whether it be perceived as good or bad. Without ultimate justice, man could possibly exercise cruelty instead of kindness. Instead of helping the old lady to cross the street, a man could rob her and take her purse.

The revealed truths of the Scriptures declare differently when they declare the moral imperative to flee from the wrath to come (Luke 3:7). Such is a call to repentance or moral conversion. God is just to judge men and to execute punishment based on the deeds that they do, based on their real and substantial guilt before Him. He is the one who commanded them to do what is right. He is Lord and must judge the deeds of His servants. Since He has undeniably spoken moral reality into being, all people rightly must answer to Him. This is the doctrine of accountability (Rom 14:12).

It may be quipped, "God may be just to send people to Hell, but God cannot be just if He keeps people in Hell." The conditionalist may dismiss themselves here but at the cost of a clear reading of the revealed truth, as we have seen. This is human pride speaking and attempting to set limits on how much God can or cannot judge man's sin. They do so with limited knowledge and little wisdom in the face of the all-knowing and all-wise God over all. This ignorance is akin to the logic that says that God should not be able to judge the sin of man at all, as seen above.

The guilty do not set their own terms of punishment, the law and its giver does. Remember how, if asked, the guilty child molester will declare the need of light punishment on those that might commit such crimes. The guilty sinner lacks the moral qualifications to limit punishment. How can an unjust man dictate to a just God how justice is allowed to go? The rapist is not free to set for himself a light sentence when justice demands a heavy one.

God is just to punish sin without limits set by the guilty conscience. As Lord, vengeance belongs solely to Him (Rom 12:19, Ps 94:1). There is a retributive justice, an eye for an eye, that has been clearly revealed to sinful men by the one true God (Ex 21:23–25). God taking vengeance against sin is the greatest expression of His justice, which is the standard for any understanding of justice as a concept.

There is a weight to our guilt that we do not adequately perceive since we neither have the right sense of morality, nor the sufficient understanding to rightly weigh. How great is our guilt for which we must be righteously adjudicated? If I steal from a man, I can repay that debt (an eye for an eye) by returning that which was stolen with interest. My wrong incurred a measurable debt. However, sin is not a crime against man alone but against God; a transgression of eternal law. It, therefore, carries an immeasurable debt. Sin affronts every eternal attribute of God. So the door to eternal justice is opened (Ps 51:4). To again invoke the popular verbiage of Sproul, it is cosmic rebellion.

If man freely chooses to transgress against the infinite holiness of God, then they would indeed have immeasurable guiltiness that demands justice. An attack on a king carries further threats of punishment than the attack on a fellow citizen. An eye for an eye is weighed differently at the final judgment than it could be in this life, especially in the eyes of the all-righteous and all-wise God. If man is wholly responsible for his deeds, then God is just to judge.

"Now," says the man in the dishonesty of his heart, "I am not responsible for my deeds. God is, therefore, unjust to judge." Such was the foolish argument that Paul attempted to answer (Rom 9:19). The free moral agency of humanity is one of the greatest apologetics for the existence of Hell. God gave man creaturely freedom to choose what he most desired, though providentially and thankfully God constrains them in His kindness. God has compelled no one to choose sin, but man has freely chosen sin from the beginning. God has restrained evil choices or used them for greater divine ends, but the responsibility for the choice of sin has always lied at the feet of the unjust men.

God is just in the condemnation of the unjust. And if Hell is the filthy being decreed to be filthy still, then they remain justly condemned in perpetuity without repentance (Rev 22:11). The unlimited fatalism argument that man is not free flies in the face of what we all know by our experience and what is declared to be true by God. The universal experience of guilt and endless desire to justify our actions tells us plainly that we engage in our sin freely. This form of fatalism attempts to excuse the individual from reality in a childish game of moral buck-passing.

Materialistic philosophy attempts to come to the treasonous aid of the rebels and tell them that only the material world exists, reducing them to machines or bundles of natural causes, unable to choose anything. They cannot explain why these hapless chemical reactions tend toward lies and larceny, toward rape and murder, toward hatred and malice, toward cruelty and envy, toward pride and blasphemy. Their godless philosophy will be of little worth to them when the judge of all examines them by His law. The soul, that thing their philosophy denies, that sins shall die (Ezek 18:20). A swinging pendulum makes no moral choices, but man is not a swinging pendulum. Thefts are not caused by the allergy of addiction but from one's own heart's desire. We are not driven by our DNA but by the lust in our heart (James 1:13–15). We are not products of our environment or determined by social forces. Despite the pressures of the culture, we know intuitively and biblically that the Nazi soldier was culpable. To allow the sociologist to draw their tree of causation showing evil outcomes as naturally springing from some mono-variant cause like poverty or racism is foolhardy. Not all born in poverty share in the evil outcomes. Not every victim of prejudice becomes a criminal. There is no discernible cause and effect relationship. There is only a discernible guilt to each perpetrator and that guilt will be obvious under the scrutiny of the great Judge of all.

The argument for the un-responsibility of mankind takes a more limited form. It is argued that since some men have not heard the Gospel of Christ, they cannot, therefore, be held responsible for rejecting God. This is a faulty notion about what makes man guilty. Men do not deserve Hell because of their ability to hear the Gospel and reject it. Men will be in Hell because of the guilt of their sin. They had opportunity to do evil and chose to do so. The knowledge of God, His existence and His wrath or judgment, is universal (Rom 1:18–20). There is natural knowledge of God and His law that is against each sinful choice. If man was innocent, this argument would carry weight. A death row inmate, not knowing that he could petition the governor for pardon, is nonetheless worthy of death if justly convicted.

Being aware of God and His commandments and becoming guilty before Him makes them subjects of His judgment.

Paul argued that men knew God but glorified Him not as God and went on to commit acts of evil (Rom 1:21–32). Any honest person will admit that they know what is right and wrong and that they have chosen to do wrong anyway, regardless of whether they have heard the Gospel or not. There are no innocent people, and there are no honest seekers of God that have been rejected by God. All men know that they are guilty. All men have the light of God and show that they prefer darkness (John 3:18–21). The Muslim born in a Muslim country may commonly become a Muslim and may likely never hear the Gospel (though that could be argued to the contrary). But that same man will still sin against the light he has. No one goes to Hell because they are Muslim or any other label that may be attached to them. They go to Hell because they are sinners by choice. They are still responsible for their sins and will remain so when justly condemned by God.

Appealing against God's justice does nothing to negate the reality of Hell as the exercise of God's justice. The rebel then turns to the claim that Hell is contrary to the love and mercy and goodness of God. The Problem of Evil argument is the last refuge for the guilty to escape from culpability. "Would a good God send people to Hell? Would a loving and merciful God keep people in Hell?" This objection tugs on our heart's strings. If Hell is real, and God assuredly declares it so, then it is a place of conscious and perpetual suffering. How does that show us the love, mercy, and goodness of God?

Admittedly, we who are committed to Christ struggle in the face of these objections. To point out that this objection is emotional and not rational does little to take the seemingly sharp edge off the doctrine. We know that our present feelings may change in the future when we have a greater understanding given to us from God. One of the themes of the Psalms is the righteous rejoicing at the judgment of the wicked, which speaks to this matter. We rightly say that until we have that greater understanding we must commit ourselves as Christians to believing what God has plainly said about this issue in the text of Scripture. He knows and will give us greater insight in the future but for now the sharp edge of the truth is still there. The discussion of justice in all its rationality that has been hitherto highlighted seems to melt away for many of us here. We have sympathy for those who we know are suffering, and that is a good thing. As such, the thought of someone suffering continually naturally stirs in us a wish for relief of that suffering on their behalf, even if that suffering is not a present reality.

Knowing that the emotional appeal carries some weight, most of the popular arguments against Hell sidestep the matter of justice to highlight the emotional appeal. "How can you even enjoy heaven with the knowledge of others enduring a state of suffering." The justice of Hell is not here challenged, but the emotional response of the Christian is questioned. One could answer that question a hundred different ways and still be left with the emotional impact of suffering being allowed to continue. One may say, "Our tears will be wiped away, and the former things will no more be remembered." But the emotional impact remains. Will we have a more perfect understanding of the fate and state of the lost? No doubt we will, but others still suffer. The fact that they are reduced to something less than what we knew, having no semblance of goodness left in them (the work of art that they were in the image of God in which they were created is lost), may help. We do not continually weep over the ashes of lost works of art; we accept the loss and find joy in something else. They are no longer that which we knew and loved. Such apologetic insights may carry some value, but the value of the emotional appeal remains.

"Why does God in mercy not bring it to an end?" Sound logical answers offered by faithful apologists seem cold and indifferent to that reality. "God is honoring their will." "God is not allowing the preciousness of their consciousness to extinguish." What will these arguments from human reasoning accomplish in the eyes of those gripped by the emotions of it all? The only sure answer is what we know by faith in God's word.

There remains, then, the fact of suffering. Our empathy remains too, despite the soundness of our theology. We must answer the emotional question. The emotional question is not about the existence of Hell or the justice of it, but about the apparent callousness of it. God is still good, loving, and merciful with the existence of Hell. Hell does not exclude those truths. We note that Hell was not for man but entered first because of the devil (Matt. 25:41). It was a packaged deal with sin and death. Hell was enlarged by the sin of man in his innocence (Isa 5:14). If man was not a sinner, Hell would not be discussed. If we were to single out a small frame of a man foaming out with fear and resisting in terror the arms of those that carried them to their violent death, we would feel heartfelt compassion for that man and absolute indignation against those that carried him to that end. That frame or picture illustrates our limited finite perspective. If we were able to zoom out and see the whole of the guilt of that man now foaming with fear and see his life of murder and rape and know that he was justly condemned to that end, if we in a moment could see all the broken people hurt by his unfeeling malice, we would see the picture much differently. It is sinners, vile sinners, who go forth into God's judgment. Our emotions are rarely well informed.

The original creation, which includes man, was an expression of the goodness of God. Before sin, God declared all of creation to be very good. Sin caused Hell to be, not God. We are to blame for Hell, and not God. Hell is for those who despise the goodness of God. They despise the goodness of God that leads them to repentance (a goodness that all men apparently experience), to embrace all forms of lust and malice (Rom 2:4). In this sense, Hell is not about the love of God at all; Hell is about the hatred of man for God, His goodness, and the good things He made. They desired autonomy from God and autonomy from God, in a greater and more permanent sense, is what they will have. It is the final eternal expression of man not willing to be reconciled to God who has done all to reconcile them to Himself (II Cor. 5:17–21). Our emotions on this matter are more than just ill-informed. They are wrong headed. They hated the just one in favor of the murderer. They desired Barabbas instead of Christ. Their objection mistakenly questions God instead of questioning man.

In addition, the goodness and love of God are not separated from His righteousness. His judgment and wrath against sin is an expression of His love and goodness. God so loved the saved that He would not allow sin, uncleanness, and hatred to enter into His eternal rest prepared for their fellowship. Hell is an eternal memorial of that hideous thing which God would not allow to enter into Heaven. Our emotions would have us bring the snake into the children's room or bring the rapist into the room of the vulnerable and innocent. God in His good judgment holds them in their own place. Because He loves, He judges.

The assumption of the scoffer is that God is aloof and malevolent to the sufferings of Hell. They picture God as separated from what they already consider, without warrant, to be unjust suffering. They envision God to be like a Caesar surveying the circus games or a Nazi resting in comfort while a starving Jew is beaten. Nothing could be further from the truth. David said that if he had made his bed in hell, God would still be there (Ps. 139). God is never separated from those whom He judges. While He is eternally angry with the wicked, this does not negate the fact that He takes no pleasure in their death, which includes the second death of the wicked

(Ezek 33:11). In a sense, if God is eternally present in the exercise of His wrath, then God is also eternally displeased with their fate.

This enters into a truth that is hard for us to understand. There will apparently be a grief that God bears in the exercise of His judgment. This is not malevolence at all. God is not sadistic. We should be mindful in correcting popular views of Hell that describe it as persons being sadistically tortured. That is not a biblical description, but they are rather descriptions that are the product of poetic and artistic license. Hell is separation from any experience or tacit knowledge of the mercy, grace, love, and comforting presence of God forever. It is described as a state of torment and not as a place of torture. It is a place where the sinner receives the fruit of their own way (Prov 1:30–32), where they continue in their malicious sinfulness, separated from the mercy and goodness of the very God they despised (Rev 22:11). An unscriptural description of Hell negates the reality of God's displeasure with this end. A sadistic guard may delight in carrying the guilty to the gallows as they do their death dance, but a just God in grief passes His judgment on the guilty. He is not aloof and indifferent. He is a merciful God who judges those who spit on His mercy.

Nothing expresses the displeasure of God with His judgment upon sin more than the suffering of God upon the cross of Christ. One cannot consider Hell without speaking of the cross. God is acquainted with the suffering of Hell. Is Hell sorrow? Christ is the Man of Sorrows (Isa 53:1–3). Is Hell where the worm dies not? Christ was made to cry, "I am a worm and no man" when He suffered on the cross (Ps 22:6). Is Hell darkness? The sun hid its face from the cross as Christ hung there (Matt 27:45). Did the rich man thirst when he was tormented in Hell? Christ cried from the sufferings of the cross, "I thirst." (John 19:28) Is Hell separation from God? Christ cried out what every sinner should cry, "My God, My God, why have you forsaken me." (Ps 22:1, Matt 27:46) Christ, as God made flesh, experienced all the horrors of Hell while He hung there, bled, and died. That is not a calloused or indifferent God. What emotional or logical arguments against God judging the sinner do we have when we stand before the bleeding and dying God/Man upon the cross? Those that go into Hell do so thoroughly guilty in complete spite of the open show of God's merciful provision.

In sum, God does not in His perfect justice or mercy sit under our judgment. We rather sit under His. He is Lord. He has revealed Himself as merciful, but we cannot bind Him. He will have mercy on whom He wills (Rom 9:15). All arguments against Hell claim that we are lord over His mercy instead of Him. We want to say that we can despise His commandments and His Lordship over us, and yet without any repentance demand that He be merciful and not just in our end. But He is Lord over His mercy, and He is Lord over His judgment. He is the potter with complete freedom over what He does with His own. Who are we to challenge His Lordship by challenging the goodness of His justice. He has declared the ends and has, in His mercy, called all men to repent (Acts 17:26–31). If we continue in sin, we will stand before Him in His justice. In rebellion against the Lord and His commandments, no one will stand before the Lord of glory with any objections or arguments against His judgment. Every mouth will then be stopped.

Chapter 5

Hell is the Fearful End Yet to Come on the Sinner

"And death and hell were cast into the lake of fire. This is the second death."

REVELATION 20:14

"But the fearful, and unbelieving, and the abominable, and murderers, and whoremongers, and sorcerers, and idolaters, and all liars, shall have their part in the lake which burneth with fire and brimstone: which is the second death."

REVELATION 21:8

Forasmuch then as the children are partakers of flesh and blood, he also himself likewise took part of the same; that through death he might destroy him that had the power of death, that is, the devil; And deliver them who through fear of death were all their lifetime subject to bondage."

HEBREWS 2:14, 15

HELL IS NOT A present but an eschatological truth. It does not exist here and now but will exist then and there. It is not of this world but of the world to come. It is preached that men may now flee from it and escape it. In this sense, Hell is intended now to be its own deterrent and intended to induce the sinner to turn to their God. For now, the subject of Hell is a mercy to any who hear it, contrary to the charge that it is hateful and mean-spirited. God asked the sinner, "As I live, saith the Lord God, I have no pleasure in the death of the wicked; but that the wicked turn from his way and live: turn ye, turn ye from your evil ways; for why will ye die, O house of Israel?" (Ezek 33:11) Hear now the question God has asked, "Why will you die?" Now is the time of mercy, but that time will one day come to a close. As those dying of the snake bite were bidden to look and live (Num 21:8, John 3:14), any who refused to look would die. Why would they die? The truly blind are those who refuse to look toward this truth, and the truly unmerciful are those who refuse to speak of it.

Earlier, the allegory of the death row inmate was invoked, and here it would be helpful to see the allegory more fully as it relates to the eschatological truth of the Scriptures. As long as the inmate in his guilt remains in the cell, he may seek pardon, express contrition, and hope that something will change in his circumstance to prevent his execution. There is no guarantee that mercy will be extended, but the moment will come when the guards come and lead the one to be executed to their execution. The time to seek mercy is present and not afterward. Despite the inmate's death dance of desperation, the guards will bring them to the place of death, and the sentence of death will be carried out. We may call the time between the condemnation and the execution the time of mercy.

Unlike this allegory, our reality has the final judge and governor saying to the wicked in their cell, "Why will you die?" But the picture is the same. Men rebelled against the Lord and were brought under the penalty of death (Rom 5:12). They remain there under the penalty of death, not executed yet. Man fears this death and knows in the depths of their conscience it is a reality that one day must come. They ". . . through fear of death were all their lifetime subject to bondage." (Heb 2:15) They are held in chains, fearfully waiting for the execution. The time will come for the guards, the angels, to take the wicked to the fires of Hell (Matt 13:41, 42, 49, 50). The place they go is called death (Rev 20:14, 21:8). It will be final, complete, and irrevocable. The time of mercy will be passed.

Death and its finality hang over sinful mankind. Man may vainly try to ignore it or try to defeat it figuratively by doing things to be remembered or physically by trusting in health fads or the false promises of science to extend their present lives indefinitely. No matter what they do, death remains their fearful end. Under the threat of death, many will give themselves over to the pleasures of sin in hopes of dulling the painful thought. Others will embrace religion and philosophies that give them false hope that death is only a cycle to a new beginning. Most will try to minimize its meaning by saying that death is the end of existence (i.e., cessation) instead of an eschatological end. The Scriptures offer the only true and revealed view of the reality of death, and what it ultimately answers to is the reality of Hell, or final judgment.

While the conditionalist is right in saying that the man as a creature is not immortal and depends on continued life from the source of life, which is God alone, this creatureliness is not the all-encompassing truth of the nature of death. What do we know by God's revelation? We know that the soul (i.e., the spiritual reality or life of the person, whatever its nature and relationship to the body might be) outlives the body and we know of no revelation that speaks of its end. Instead, we know that the body is destined to be raised and reunited with the soul. Whether in Heaven or Hell, there is an open-ended continuing of life in both. This leads to a needed look at the nature of death and its relationship to final judgment. Ultimately, in what way is Hell synonymous with death?

Death is one of the greatest of all philosophical questions, the great unknown, the undiscovered country, and is considered by some to be the underlying problem of all philosophical inquiry. It is in one sense certain that we all must die and, in another sense, it is mysterious, for we know not when and how death may come or what change it will bring. Death is the great unknown, at least from the finite perspective of the creature. We are all afraid to die, and it is only great experiences of pain that cause a person to seek or desire death. Death becomes the chief driving force of what people do and why they do it, "Let us eat, drink, and be merry; for tomorrow we die." (I Cor 15:32) It teaches us that the Lordship of God is over our lives. Our life is not ours, for we cannot control when or how death comes. Some foolish souls, like Hemmingway, in order to exert their belief that they are masters of their own fate, have taken their own lives. What does it gain then, but a loss of all the perceived autonomy they professed, for now they are nothing in this world? Suicide is an attempt to exert foolish autonomy, at least for the existential philosopher. That is why philosophers like Sartre and Camus made the question of suicide the final philosophical question, for control over death is the thing man cannot master. As our culture has denied the Lordship of God, we have become a suicidal culture of death. Our culture, like others before it, with foolhardiness, believes that they will be the ones to master death. Yet the daily illnesses and obituaries prove that death continues mockingly to master them. As it was in Dostoevsky's *The Possessed*, Kirillov would prove to be a madman before his suicide and our nihilistic culture must show itself mad before it finally dies.

Death informs ethics. If we die and are no more, as some teach, we must wrestle with the question of why we should not do as we please in this life. Our view of death informs our metaphysics. It speaks to the ultimate questions of meaning, value, and destiny. Death confronts us with all of those realities. Funerals become conduits for philosophical introspection for every average Joe. It speaks of the power of God over us, for none of us can add a moment to our life, no matter our station. It is the great equalizer of all men. The worms will eat the rich and poor alike. It speaks of the overall frailty and vanity of our nature; whatever we accomplish we will leave behind when death comes.

Death also speaks of the duality of our nature in that it speaks of the essence of life. Life is more than the functions of the body. The human being is more than the sum of its parts. There is a force of life that cannot be measured. There is a will in man that, when gone, robs the body of life. It tells us, above all, that our life is not our own, as already stated. We did not give ourselves life and we cannot retain our life at our own will. If robbed of breath, our will to breathe becomes meaningless. Therefore, there is a power above us that may and will demand our lives. God gives life. When God removes His spirit or breath, we return to dust (Ps. 104:29).

But how do we define death? How do we draw boundaries for this undiscovered country? To understand the meaning of death, we must know the meaning of life. What is life's essence? What is it ontologically? On the biological level, something is alive when the cells are dividing and generating further living cells, which is an astounding and astonishing phenomenon, mysterious in and of itself, beyond the explanatory power of materialistic evolution. This biological reality speaks of all plant and animal life. In the Septuagint, the words translated "living soul" in reference to mankind are the same words translated "living creature" on all other animal life created on day five and day six of creation. If it was not for the special relationship that God made with man in creation (i.e., created in His own image and was directly involved in forming man as opposed to speaking the creative word alone), then there would be no difference between mankind and all the rest of the creatures. It is the vertical relationship to God that makes man different from the rest of creation. There is a greater existential dimension to what it means to be alive from the human perspective. We know that our life is fundamentally different from plant and even animal life. A biological description of life only speaks of the process of maintaining life. It describes the how of life and not its essence. It can tell us nothing of how life began, what it means, or what its nature is.

Life is activity. Life is self-replicating. It grows and feeds and produces offspring. All of these are what life does, but not what life is. These descriptions separate organic material from the inorganic material such as rocks, but they are unable to tell us the difference between organic material and chemical reactions like fire, which appear to do all the same things. Life is more than chemical reactions, but it involves a unique awareness of itself and things outside itself.

There are greater forms of life and lesser forms of life. The modern assumption is that all higher forms of life evolved from lower forms of life, but the source of life is still unknown in such musings. What is its source? Life did not arise spontaneously or from nothing. The laws of biogenesis tell us that life produces life and produces similar life. If we do not begin with life as the first and efficient cause, then we can never have the existence of life at all.

What then is life? God is life (John 1:4). He is the living God (Ps 18:47). He is perfect in consciousness and in relationship to Himself. He eternally is active and has eternally begotten life in Himself (the Son and the Spirit). He created life in the reality that we know, as a product of Himself. He created man, the crown of His creation, in His own image and breathed into them the breath of life. Thus, we live and move and have our being (Acts 17:28). Therefore, life is that force and activity that is in God, and as such can exist in the things that He created. Life is not an evolving thing, but the infinite and immutable existence of God who acts in full self-awareness and in reciprocal relationship within His own nature (i.e., the persons of the Trinity). He imparted or communicated that very thing in His creation in lesser but reflective ways; a world teaming with life to His glory and honor. Through God alone we know what life is, for He revealed Himself, and there is no other explanation for life other than the immortality of the living God (I Tim 6:16).

Knowing that God is life, we now are able to ascertain what death is. Death is that which is deprived of the life and care of God. God withdraws His presence and the flowers wither and die. "You hide your face, they are troubled: You take away their breath, they die, and return to their dust. You

send forth your spirit, they are created: and You renew the face of the earth."
(Ps 104:29, 30)

The Scriptures teach that life is fleeting outside of the immortality of God. What is life as to the creature in this present world? Life is a vapor that appears for a short time and vanishes away (James 4:14). Such is the life absent of God as its ethical end. When defining terms, the word "death" is one of the most misunderstood words. It is commonly falsely defined as the cessation of being. But it is never scripturally described as such. In God we have our being (Acts 17:28), and as exegeted by Christ, at least for Abraham, Isaac, and Jacob, being is continually given by God beyond the grave (Mark 12:26, 27). In the face of any texts that appear to declare the contrary, the burden would be on the conditionalist to demonstrate that death encompasses God bringing the end of any being. God could will an end of being, but has He declared that He has or ever would?[1]

God first introduced the concept of death as a warning to man against sin (Gen 2:17). It remains forever connected with sin (Rom 6:23). God told Adam that on the day he disobeyed he would die. That day came. Adam did not cease to be or exist in that moment. There was no cessation of being that was described in the revelation of God in the first death. There is a sense that, in His mercy and longsuffering, God has withheld His judgment and, rather, made a way of salvation, but that does not fully answer the surety of the command and its promised result when broken. "Do not eat from it, when you do you will die."

The day Adam took of the fruit, two changes happened which are indicative of death. First, man hid from God immediately. Second, and ultimately, man was driven by God from the garden and barred from entering into the presence of God again. Both were the immediate and ultimate consequences of man taking the fruit. These are forms of separation. There was a spiritual and psychological separation, and then there followed an actual physical separation. The first death was that man hid himself from God and the second death, which answers to the second death for all eternity, was that God told man to depart from Him in judgment.

This is not to say that God's force and activity ceased to sustain the life of man, but He ceased rather to relate to man in terms of special favor. They were not separated from His sustaining power but were from His personal presence. Those who do not know God now (experiencing the first death,

---

1. Note: references to the dead not knowing anything (Ecc 9:5) speak only to their relationship to this world and not to their continued existence, as Christ Himself highlighted.

hiding themselves from Him in their sin) will be separated from Him forever one day (in the second death of the final judgment). There became a
wall of separation between man and God. God was the source of the life of
man. It was by God that man became a living thing. Now, separate from
God, man became a dead thing. Thus, God has defined for us the concept
of death.

The view of death set forth in the first few chapters of Genesis sets
the stage for how it is understood throughout the whole of the Scriptures.
Death can be considered in three distinct lights: physical death (death
that deals with separation from this present world), spiritual death (death
that deals with the nature of the those who are described as being without
Christ), and the most controversial of all, the second death (how the scriptures describe the lot of those who do not know Christ in the world yet to
come).

Death has reigned since the fall of man (Rom 5:14). From an evolu-
tionary point of view, life arose from death and conflict, and death is built
into reality. Death and suffering in a system absent the Living God becomes
the mechanism of change and progress toward nothing. Biblically speaking, though, death is a relational term to describe how the creature relates
to its Creator.

The existence of death is seen as an invader to man's reality in scriptural terms; One that entered due to sin (Rom 5:12). Sin and its consequence, death, came upon us all through our federal or representative head,
Adam. This affected all of creation over which Adam presided in his crown-
ing rule over creation.[2] All creation now groans under this world of death
and suffering (Rom 8:20–22). The scriptural view is that, being dead, man
marches toward the second and final death of which physical death is a type
and shadow. This present time will end and the world to come will begin.
Physical death is the shadow of the reality of the creature's relationship to
its Creator. The fifth chapter of Genesis teaches that the lot of humanity is to
live under the sun for an uncertain amount of time and then die, or as the
curse said, to return to the dust from whence we came (Gen 3:19).

Fear of death is the evidence that all men have an innate knowledge
that there is judgment beyond the grave. It is not the fear of oblivion that
scares us. It is the fear of judgment and the unknown reality that we must

2. While some form of death and decay occurred as part of the natural created order—the second law of thermodynamics, the consumption of energy, the processing of
food, maybe even the natural food chain—though not as savage as it exists under the
curse, etc.—Death and suffering as we know it now was foreign to that world.

yet face. We are headed somewhere. Men distinctly know that when they die there will be a form of continuance. They know that some form of justice awaits them. The Scriptures clearly declare this innate knowledge of men to be true. There is an appointment for all men already set, and after this is the judgment (Heb 9:27). There is an "after this" reality and no one is ignorant of it. There is appointed physical life and physical death once for all, and then a judgment. Again, physical death is not described as the end or cessation of being. There is something after it. After it dies, that same being is met with an actual judgment. This is not contrary to our observation of God's world. We have seen things move from one state to another, but we have never seen anything cease to be. Something may be reduced to ashes, but it does not cease to be. The Scriptures likewise are opposed to the idea of cessation. Rather, the concept of separation is the scriptural definition of death in all its forms.

As for physical death, it is not the end of any individual, but something that occurs to the soul or life of man in its relationship to this physical world. The positive description of death in the Scriptures is that it is the separation of the soul (the spiritual aspect of man) from the body (the physical aspect of man). The soul, which is the life God breathed into the body of man, departs the body at death. The body is deprived of the life and care of God. Separated from the soul, it disintegrates into dust (not non-existence).

Physical death speaks to the duality of man's nature. It tells of the life of man and its connection to the world and the body/soul duality. The Scriptures declare that when physical death occurs the breath, spirit, or ghost (again that which was imparted to man by God) separates from the body (Gen 25:17; 35:18, 29; 49:33; Job 3:11; Matt 27:50; Mark 15:37, 39; Luke 23:46; John 19:30; Acts 5:5, 10; 12:23; etc.). The dust returns to the earth, and the spirit returns to God that made it (Ecc 12:7).

Christ upheld this duality by stating that one should not fear those that can only kill the body, but should fear only God who could destroy both body and soul in Hell (Matt 10:28). There may be little room for the existence of the soul in modernity and in empiricism as a philosophy of knowledge, but it is a revelational fact that we all intuitively know. A materialistic view cannot account for human consciousness, among other things. We are more than chemical reactions. Unconscious material or matter cannot produce consciousness, intelligence, volition, or sensibility.

Man has a will. Where is the will located? Man has emotions. Where are they located? Man has rationality and free thought. Where does it lie? We could take ourselves apart piece by piece, but we could never find a part or a single cell of which we could say "here is what they believe" or "here is what they feel about such." Our brains receive and transmit our will to the members and if the brain is damaged, consciousness is altered. However, our will, emotions, and intelligence that make up our consciousness and personality are not identical with our bodily existence. It is above it, behind it, and intimately connected with it, but the soul is not the body. Our everyday language betrays our belief that we are more than the sum of our parts. We say "my hand" or "my body" without thought about what the personal pronoun "my" refers to.

The Scriptures are uniform on this matter. Physical death is the separation of the body and the soul, and resurrection is the reunion of the body and soul. The original and eschatological end of man proclaims this duality. The material reality of man is made up of the very elements of the earth. All of that material can be present, yet man is not living. God breathed into his nostrils and man became something more than the material; a living creature in the image of God (Gen 2:7). A spiritual reality connected to this world through a physical body is what man is as created by God. We are connected to this world through the body given to us by God. Paul described the soul as the inward man, which is renewed day by day as opposed to the body which is perishing (II Cor 4:16). Paul, speaking about his revelations, could not tell whether the experiences were in the body or out of the body (II Cor 12:2). There is a clear distinction between the soul and the body, though the ability to discern them outside of revelation is difficult (Heb 4:12). The body and soul are not intended to be separated. The body is the house of the soul, its tent or sheath (II Cor 5:1, II Pet 1:13). God "forms the spirit of man within him." (Zech 12:1)

Scriptures also declare a continued consciousness exists after death, that is, between physical death and resurrection. The words of Christ concerning those that physically died in the Old Covenant are sufficient here. "God is not the God of the dead, but of the living." (Matt 22:32) Therefore, Christ stated that Abraham and Isaac and Jacob, whose bodies were still in the grave, lived, and God was yet their God. Christ again declared to the thief on the cross, "Today shalt thou be with me in Paradise." (Luke 23:43) When Christ died, His death was described as His human soul separating from His human body (Mark 15:37, Luke 23:46, John 19:30). His body went to the tomb, but His soul was with the thief in Paradise that very same day. Paul, speaking of his own death, described it as being a departure where he immediately expected to be with Christ (Phil 1:23, 24, II Tim 4:6). He continued to describe death in these terms, "to be absent from the body, and to present with the Lord." (II Cor 5:8)

Physical death is the sleep of the body absent the soul. When speaking of the resurrection to life or to shame, Daniel said that those who sleep in the dust will awake (Dan 12:2). Paul encouraged the Thessalonians that those who have died in Christ, who are said to be asleep, were yet to be raised up with Christ (I Thess 4:13–15). Physical death carries the idea of the sleep of the body and the continuance of the soul, and not the non-existent state of either. The believer, once rescued from death, is said to never die (John 11:26). Physical death is not the real death. Sleep speaks of ceasing from labor in rest. Sleep speaks of continuing life. Sleep speaks of an expectation of awakening. It is fitting to use as a description of the Christian hope, and thus, in the New Covenant the term sleep is applied especially to the physical death of believers. As with Lazarus, Christ will come one day to awake them.

The body and the spirit have two different temporary destinations at the point of physical death. The body is said to go back to the earth as it was, but the spirit is said to return to the God that gave it (Ecc 12:7). Peter, looking forward to his own death, describes it by saying, "I must put off this my tabernacle. . . ." (II Pet 1:13, 14) We cannot take this in a gnostic sense as a renouncement of the physical body. The body was a good creation of God. It is that which connects us to this God-created world. It is our hands that carry the Bible. It is our feet that take us to the fields. It is our tongues that preach the Gospel to a lost and dying world. Our bodies belong to God, are the dwelling places of the Holy Spirit, and may be accepted by God as living sacrifices (I Cor 6:19, 20, Rom 12:1–2). However, in physical death we must put off these bodies for a time. And this state, while not yet perfect, is glorious for the believer. Paul stated to the Philippians that he had a longing for death so he could be with Christ (Phil 1:22–24).

The truth of physical death leads to the hope of resurrection for the believer and to the fear of resurrection for the non-believer. This is central and unique to the Christian faith, which is based on the real and historical resurrection of Christ from the dead. We believe that Christ Jesus literally died, and He literally rose again in the same body (John 2:19–21). His risen body bore the marks of the crucifixion (John 20:27). He did this in His own power proving His deity (John 10:18). We will be like our risen Lord and the pattern of His resurrection (I John 3:1, 2). Our risen body will go from dishonor to glory, from corruption to incorruption, and from mortality to immortality (I Cor 15:42–54).

Going back to the matter of sleep and its relationship to the hope of resurrection. There is a declaration in the Scriptures that the bodies of the saints that slept arose (Matt 27:52). That text explained to us what sleeping is. It is the body waiting for an awakening. Consider Christ raising the young maid back to life (Luke 8:52–56). There is a reunion of the soul and body fully described with the words "And her spirit came again. . . ." It is the reverse of what takes place at physical death. The soul and body reunite, for whole man is both in union. This is further illustrated with the two witnesses in Revelation (Rev 11:11).

Physical death is not the totality of our understanding of death, but it is a type or shadow of it. It is not even the real death described from the beginning, which is the immediate change that happened to man in his relationship to His God when he sinned. Death is a spiritual reality that speaks to man's relationship with the Living God. Adam was the pattern of the real death that came upon all men. He died the moment he ate the fruit. That is the reality of us all. In Adam, where all of humanity was residing at that time and who represented us all perfectly, all die (I Cor 15:22).

We all experienced this death, for we all became sinners separated from God in the sin of Adam (Isa 59:2, Rom 5:12). Death is the righteous judgment on the sinfulness of man. Paul tells us in his letter to the Ephesians that, before God had grace toward us, we were dead in our sins (Eph 2:1–5). This is the real death already experienced by all. The real death is not ceasing to be, it is sin as the point of separation between God and us (Eph 2:12–14). When the prodigal son came home from the far country to be with his father, his father cried out for joy that his son who was dead was now alive (Luke 15:24). He was dead because he was separated from his father.

In Adam, all in sin are dead and under condemnation already (John 3:18). In their sinfulness, they are hiding from the presence of God as Adam was and one day (absent reconciliation) are under threat of being driven from God's presence with finality. That is the first death and the abiding death that shapes the reality of mankind.

But there is yet a death to come that belongs to any who die in their sins unreconciled to God (John 8:24). This death has been canceled for those who live in Christ and believe in Him, for they will never die (John

11:25, 26). The second or final death is the execution of the condemnation of sinful men. It is not to a nonexistent state just as any other consideration of death is not thus.[3] In the end, we are left to God's disposal (Ecc 12:7). There will be a judgment of the dead. Death and Hell will be delivered up including the dead that are in them (Rev 20:11–15). Those that belong to the realm of the dead (dead in sins) will stand in the final place of judgment to be driven away from God's grace just as Adam was from the garden and tree of life.

The first death is that which was experienced by Adam and known by all of us by virtue of sin. The second death is the judgment that one must forever remain in that state. In His justice, God must cry out "Depart from me" (Matt 25:41), for His true and unchangeable word declared that man must die for sin. There is no destruction or cessation of being spoken of. It is everlasting punishment (Matt 25:46). It is everlasting contempt (Dan 12:2). It is where the worm does not die and the fire is not quenched (Mark 9:43–48).

Therefore, we must preach it. We must tell people to flee to Christ so that they can escape the eternal wrath of God. The second death is separation, not the cessation of being. "And the smoke of their torment ascends up forever and ever: and they had no rest day nor night. . . ." (Rev 14:11) Nothing is consumed in the fire of God (Ex 3:2). If man rejects Christ, how can they escape the damnation of Hell (Matt 23:33)? There remains nothing for them but the "blackness of darkness forever" (Jude 1:13). It is justice exacted, the wages of sin is death (Rom 6:23).

What we fear about death is the reality of this final judgment. All our lives we are held in bondage to that fear, and it shapes us. We know ourselves to be under the suspension of that judgment even now. It hangs over our heads like a crushing boulder ready to drop. You must be judged. We are condemned already, and our conscience bears witness to that fact. However, though we live under the suspended sentence, we live under the reality that our God has called us to repentance and life. The just and holy God for now says, "Why will you die" (Ezek 33:11)? If we ignore Him, how shall we escape (Heb 2:3)?

---

3. Note: an example of this is the believer being called to account themselves as dead to sin, in the sense of being separated from it power (Rom 6).

Chapter 6

Hell Is the Declared End to Be Avoided

"But when he saw many of the Pharisees and Sadducees come to his baptism, he said unto them, O generation of vipers, who hath warned you to flee from the wrath to come?"

MATTHEW 3:7

THE MESSAGE OF HELL is a gracious and merciful declaration. Though that seems counterintuitive to say, in reality there is no other way to see it. It is presented as a reality not yet realized and as something that God implores men to turn away from. This perspective is lost on the rebellious, who declare that God is some kind of narcissistic, cosmic bully that tells them to love Him or He will throw them into Hell. We have already seen Hell is the symbol of God's justice that He will administer as a wise judge in the end and that all men as sinners are under the judgment of death already. God has declared the reality of Hell not as a threat, but as a warning. God has emphatically said to the condemned, "Why will you die?" When Hell is described and asserted as a future reality, it stands in that grace of warning. God speaks to the mind and conscience of man to turn away from the coming judgment. "A prudent man foresees the evil, and hides himself: but the simple pass on, and are punished." (Prov 22:3)

The message of Hell is presented with a sense of *urgency*. The teaching of Christ in the Sermon on the Mount clearly bears out this truth. When expounding on the nature of the law and our absolute guilt under it, Christ warned of the danger of Hell fire. According to Christ, the law that says we are not to kill has wider implications than just the act but covers our speech and thoughts toward others. The law, or word of God, discerns our thoughts and the intents of our hearts (Heb 4:12). We are all presented as liable to this law, deserving of its punishment.

> "But I say unto you, that whosoever is angry with his brother without a cause shall be in danger of the judgment: and whosoever shall say to his brother, Raca, shall be in danger of the council: but whosoever shall say, Thou fool, shall be in danger of hell fire." Matthew 5:22

Christ continued to speak of things particular to that command as His dialog unfolded, highlighting the breach between man and God that occurred in the sinner who transgressed that law. No one can sin against his fellow man without sinning against God. All sin is a transgression of His law. And as such sin separates us from Him (Isa 59:2).

> "Therefore, if thou bring thy gift to the altar, and there remember that thy brother hath ought against thee; Leave there thy gift before the altar, and go thy way; first be reconciled to thy brother, and then come and offer thy gift." Matthew 5:23, 24

We cannot offer anything to God in the state of our guilt. God will not accept us in our guilt because He is holy and just. Rather, God in His justice must commit us to His wrath against sin. This is the grace and mercy of the warning declared:

> "Agree with thine adversary quickly, whiles thou art in the way with him; lest at any time the adversary deliver thee to the judge, and the judge deliver thee to the officer, and thou be cast into prison. Verily I say unto thee, thou shalt by no means come out thence, till thou hast paid the uttermost farthing." Matthew 5:25, 26

The latter part of this warning is often seized by those that hold to a restorative ideology regarding Hell (that Hell will one day end with a release of the sinner from Hell into Heaven). Like the conditionalist, they deny the endlessness of Hell but insert salvation instead of annihilation as its end.[1] The restorative doctrine is in direct contradiction to other plain texts already highlighted, other plain declarations of Christ (Luke 14:24,

---

1. Note: for this reason, it is fair to call both conditional and restorational views of Hell views of process judgment instead of final judgment. The judgement for both is not final and leads to a separate end.

Matt 12:32[2]) and carries the blasphemous idea that one's own suffering, apart from Christ, can propitiate or expiate for sins. Such a doctrine cannot sustain the message of the Scriptures. We will deal with the danger of restorational doctrine later. But for now, note that it is not necessary for an understanding of the analogy of the text. Rather, Christ offers a finite picture of a more immediate reality. The danger and liability all have regarding Hell and final judgment can be compared to the exercise of earthly justice and its demand that a full payment is made as a penalty for injustice.

The analogy leads us to the fearful truth. If one is not reconciled to God, they will experience the fullness of the punishment due. The fact that reconciliation is possible, even from the danger of Hell fire, is part of the understanding of the warning. The analogy of the need to be reconciled is told in terms one can understand. In earthly matters where you are liable in law against your brother for a real offense, if you refuse to come to reconciling terms with the brother in their lawful suit, then they are your adversary and you are in their hands. At which point they are within their legal rights to bring you before the judgment seat before a judge. That judge has power to hand you over to the officer who has the ability to cast you into prison for the full term of the punishment.

But Hell is not a temporal, but eternal reality. And one is under the warning of Hell before their God. There is this space of time under the longsuffering of God that one might do something to avoid that find judgment. We do not know how long a space of time that is allowed for any to seek reconciliation, therefore one must act quickly. If it is true with human tribunals and offenses against human laws, how much more with God's law? God receives righteous prosecution against you, is a righteous Judge over you, and may in the end command His angels to cast you away in the full execution of righteous judgment.

See this for what it is then. You are yet in the way toward final judgment. There is now a sense of urgency. Be reconciled to God. There is time now to plead, not when the adjudication is finished and the final sentence is passed down. Now is the day of salvation (II Cor 6:2). Today, do not harden your heart if you hear His voice (Heb 3:15). In essence, you can come to terms with God now. The threat of Hell is coupled with the gracious message that you can fall before Him now and may find terms of mercy. You are currently enemies of a merciful God (Rom 5:10). But that holy God may have mercy on whom He wills (Rom 9:15). There will come a day when

---

2. For some, at least, there will be no forgiveness in the world to come.

mercy will no longer be extended. "They that observe lying vanities forsake their own mercy." (Jonah 5:8)

There is not only a sense of urgency in the declaration of Hell, but also an encouragement toward *extreme resolve* in its merciful declaration. When Hell is preached it encourages repentance. The doctrine calls us to consider the cost of our sin as it is weighed against the reality of eternal condemnation and punishment. The wise will not only consider their limited space of time to be reconciled but also the price they will pay if they are not reconciled.

Christ went on in the Sermon on the Mount to speak of the law against adultery and its guilt before God, even when it occurs in the thoughts or intents of one's own heart (Matt 5:27, 28). Seeing that God takes account even of your innermost sinful desires, the warning against final judgment again surfaces.

> "And if thy right eye offend thee, pluck it out, and cast it from thee: for it is profitable for thee that one of thy members should perish, and not that thy whole body should be cast into hell. And if thy right hand offend thee, cut it off, and cast it from thee: for it is profitable for thee that one of thy members should perish, and not that thy whole body should be cast into hell." Matthew 5:29

Whatever it is that works the love of sin and prevents one from repentance from that sin is worth being cut off and cast away in order to avoid the coming wrath.

To the immediate subject, the lust of the eyes is emphasized (I John 2:15–17). There may be those whose eyes are full of idolatry (II Pet 2:14). They love to behold those things which work in their hearts all manner of concupiscence. These motions of sin are familiar to all of us in our fallen nature. We have all felt their power. That sin is dragging all men to final judgment. Christ said that it would be better for you that the right eye (that being the eye of your strength), which causes you to stumble, or rather scandalizes you, be removed completely and cast aside if that was necessary to part you from your condemning sinfulness. Your love of the sin that condemns you is not worth holding on to.

Again, in applying this beyond the subject of the lust of the eyes, Christ says that if it is the right hand (the hand of your strength) that is connected with your scandalization, then to cut it off would be preferable, if needed, to separate you from your sinfulness. The message is clear. No matter how traumatic the act of repentance is, such a radical repentance from the stronghold of your sin is presently to be preferred over the more severe condemnation yet to come against it. Any cancer patient of today or the gangrene afflicted of days gone by would immediately see the wisdom of this warning. To lose a member of the body now is preferred over losing the whole body later. God has reasoned with the lost man, asking them to compare the value of their present pleasure in things which rebel against God's commands with God's future judgment against them.

The warning of Hell is a merciful declaration calling men to turn from sin to the God that shows mercy. In the context of the Sermon on the Mount, Christ speaks to their potential profit or advantage (*sumphero*). Sin cannot profit you if you must lose all in the end for it. This is not the only instance of such a blessed warning (Matt 18:6). It is, according to Joseph Benson, "[Better] to suffer an apparent temporary loss of pleasure or profit, rather than that thy whole soul and body should perish eternally, which yet would be the fatal consequence of thy indulging a favorite lust. . . ."[3] The cancer must be cut out or the gangrene leg must be removed, or it will corrupt and kill the whole person. A merciful physician speaks in this clear manner. Paul in an indirect commentary on the words of Christ gives it a clearer sense;

> "Mortify therefore your members which are upon the earth; forni-
> cation, uncleanness, inordinate affection, evil concupiscence, and
> covetousness, which is idolatry: For which things' sake the wrath
> of God cometh on the children of disobedience." Colossians 3:5, 6

When Hell is preached, it asks all to consider what is better, the pleasure of sin for a short season or a temporary loss in repentance that escapes wrath to attain incorruptible riches.

Even stronger language is used to shake men from their self-righteousness and self-reliance. Christ, after using strong vocatives pinpointing the utter lost condition of the Pharisees, asked His enemies, "How can ye escape the damnation of hell?" (Matt 23:33) Such words mirrored the same searching question asked by the Baptist, "who hath warned you to flee from the wrath to come?" (Matt 3:7) And later the writer to the Hebrews again asked how we could escape by neglecting such a great salvation (Heb 2:3, 4). How is this a mercy? It draws men to consider those witnesses that have spoken to them already, witnesses that have gone unheeded to this point.

---

3. Benson, Joseph: *Joseph Benson's Commentary on the Old and New Testaments.*

To the Pharisees, Moses and Prophets had and continually spoke of their sin and God's coming judgment.

The possibility of turning and finding mercy has been held out to the enemies of Christ in the repeated warnings. There is a person, the "who" of the text, that has spoken and told you to flee from that wrath. The rich man in hell was told that there was a sufficient warning in Moses and the prophets that was able to keep them from that place of torment (Luke 26:28–31). That person is the Lord. It is the Lord who spoke and moved holy men of old to speak.

There is a 'how to' that has been shown to them as well, in type in the sacrifices provided by God and in the reality of the Lamb of God. There is such a great salvation and an opportunity now to flee to it from the wrath to come (Prov 18:10). In longsuffering, God has stretched out His hands to sinners. No one can say that they were not warned to flee and have not also been offered a refuge to flee to. Even those who have only the light of natural revelation have the wrath of God revealed from heaven to them and know in their conscience that they should flee from it to the truth of God (Rom 1:18–20).

Hell being declared reveals rebellion in the heart of man who will not depart from their sin and do not desire to agree with their adversary. They do not desire to fear God and will not set the fear of the Lord before their eyes (Rom 3:10–20). Christ offers up the doctrine of Hell as a reason to fear (Matt 10:28). He says in effect that we ought to fear and magnify the name of our God who is worthy. "Who will not fear you, O Lord?" (Rev 15:3, 4) The subject of Hell is intended to shake people from their complacency. God, speaking through the apostle, stated to the sinner that,

> ". . . after thy hardness and impenitent heart [you treasure] up unto thyself wrath against the day of wrath and revelation of the righteous judgment of God. . . .. unto them that are contentious, and do not obey the truth, but obey unrighteousness, indignation and wrath, Tribulation and anguish, upon every soul of man that doeth evil." Romans 2:5–9

There is a fearful end to those who will not seek the glory of God now.

Christ has asked, "How will you escape the damnation of Hell?" He asked the question after outlining the true charges against those who deemed themselves innocent, not knowing the fullness of their accountability and liability before God. They would neither admit to or repent from their sins, so He asked them how it was that they were going to escape.

"What hope do you have?" He asked them that after vocatively declaring to them their true nature, being of the rebellious serpent's seed, lost and undone, in a state of complete enmity against God and His people ("Ye serpents, ye generation of vipers"). And so He asked, "how were they going to escape?" Those strong words were a mercy to a people not yet brought before the throne of judgment. Judgment comes, and for the sinner there is a warning of it. If they ignore its warning, what hope do they have? The storm sirens are sounding, and one can now seek shelter or refuge.

Christ said in another place by way of warning that "Ye will not come to me, that ye might have life." (John 5:40) He was presenting Himself as a means of escape from death. He went on to tell them that they have Moses standing against them as an accuser against that unbelief (John 5:45–47). The context in which these truths are declared is the impending judgment that is committed to the Son (Ps 2).

> "And [The Father] hath given [The Son] authority to execute judg-
> ment also, because he is the Son of man. Marvel not at this: for the
> hour is coming in the which all that are in the graves shall hear his
> voice, and shall come forth; they that have done good, unto the
> resurrection of life; and they that have done evil, unto the resur-
> rection of damnation." John 5:27–29

Those that have done good are those coming to Him and believing on Him. Those that have done evil are those not doing so. God has made Himself and His salvation known, and like the brazen serpent has bid men to look and live (John 3:14). But they will not do so! The fullness of where they are headed is made plain to them. "Why will you die?" They are in danger of dying in their sins in the state of unbelief and Christ is shaking them with the harsh truth of Justice. Love and mercy are doing this in the proclamation of Hell.

We are reminded then that these are the words of Christ Himself. The person who has warned us was God in the flesh, tabernacled among us. It was God that has warned men of the coming judgment. "But the Lord shall endure for ever: he hath prepared his throne for judgment. And he shall judge the world in righteousness, he shall minister judgment to the people in uprightness." (Ps 9:7, 8) Since the beginning, man has been warned of sin and its consequences. There is not a man, woman, boy, or girl that has not heard the voice of God in this matter, thundering from their conscience and from the unmistakable voice of special revelation. God has told you that unless you repent you will perish as all other sinners will.

Because it is the voice of God Himself, there is a moral imperative to us all to flee from that wrath. We are morally responsible to repent and agree with our adversary. The forerunner of Christ and last Old Covenant prophet pointed men to the voice of warning and added these words;

> ". . . who hath warned you to flee from the wrath to come? Bring forth therefore fruits meet for repentance: And think not to say within yourselves, we have Abraham to *our* father: for I say unto you, that God is able of these stones to raise up children unto Abraham. And now also the axe is laid unto the root of the trees: therefore, every tree which bringeth not forth good fruit is hewn down, and cast into the fire. I indeed baptize you with water unto repentance: but he that cometh after me is mightier than I, whose shoes I am not worthy to bear: he shall baptize you with the Holy Ghost, and *with* fire: Whose fan *is* in his hand, and he will thoroughly purge his floor, and gather his wheat into the garner; but he will burn up the chaff with unquenchable fire." Matthew 3:7–12

The warning that there is a wrath to come, coupled with a graphic description of that wrath, brought forth an imperative. Bring forth fruits suitable to show repentance. All people are responsible before God to do all they can to escape that fate. Sadly, most plug their ears at the warning and go forward unchanged by the merciful God speaking to them.

Chapter 7

Hell Is the Reality that Must Be Declared

Son of man, I have made thee a watchman unto the house of Israel: therefore, hear the word at my mouth, and give them warning from me. When I say unto the wicked, thou shalt surely die; and thou gave him not warning, nor spoke to warn the wicked from his wicked way, to save his life; the same wicked man shall die in his iniquity; but his blood will I require at thine hand. Yet if thou warn the wicked, and he turn not from his wickedness, nor from his wicked way, he shall die in his iniquity; but thou hast delivered thy soul."

EZEKIEL 3:17–19

THE TREND IN THE last century in response to changing moral and theological views of culture is to set aside the seemingly negative message of wrath in order to embrace a seemingly inclusive and positive message of love. The result of this shift away from the declaration of sin, Hell, and judgment is the contemporary church lacking any imperative for calling the sinner toward repentance. The message of love becomes the de facto message of universal salvation where no one needs to turn to God from sin. The gracious message of Hell being rejected means that the merciful warning is not heard and by consequence not heeded. Sinners remained unaffected by their need of Christ. Sinners go on their way toward their end without any voice to turn them back outside of the voice of nature and conscience which has been dulled by false teachers.

Further, they become emboldened in their way. Any seldom warning against their way and the end of their sin, is dismissed as hateful and outmoded, seeing that contemporary religious instructors tell them there is no danger. Sin is allowed to fester in their heart until it affects all they touch. Culture rots as wicked men are emboldened by the message of no-judgment and no-consequences in the end. This repudiation by the current church culture of any real danger ahead for mankind absent their repentance is the most hateful, self-serving, and cowardice betrayal of humanity. But this is the kind of church the lost world demands. It hates and kills the true prophets who declare true judgment. The church must decide whether they will be faithful to their Lord or popular with the world.

Enter the true prophet and his commission. The prophet Ezekiel was commissioned by God to speak a "Thus says the Lord" message to a rebellious people, warning of their pending temporal judgment. God had determined to destroy the rebellious people as a nation and to only show mercy on the repentant. With that charge Ezekiel (as the messenger) received a warning from God. This warning, being true of a temporal judgment, applies directly to us who have a greater burden of warning to bear to rebellious mankind; a warning against final and eternal judgment.

> "Son of man, I have made thee a watchman unto the house of Israel: therefore, hear the word at my mouth, and give them warning from me. When I say unto the wicked, thou shalt surely die; and you gave him not warning, nor spoke to warn the wicked from his wicked way, to save his life; the same wicked man shall die in his iniquity; but his blood will I require at thine hand." Ezekiel 3:17, 18

This warning was so important to the ministry of Ezekiel that God would repeat it with even more vehemence later in the book:

> "Again the word of the Lord came unto me, saying, Son of man, speak to the children of thy people, and say unto them, When I bring the sword upon a land, if the people of the land take a man of their coasts, and set him for their watchman: If when he sees the sword come upon the land, he blow the trumpet, and warn the people; Then whosoever heareth the sound of the trumpet, and taketh not warning; if the sword come, and take him away, his blood shall be upon his own head. He heard the sound of the trumpet and took not warning; his blood shall be upon him. But he that taketh warning shall deliver his soul. But if the watchman see the sword come, and blow not the trumpet, and the people be not warned; if the sword come, and take any person from among

them, he is taken away in his iniquity; but his blood will I require at the watchman›s hand." Ezekiel 33:1–6

The metaphor is not complicated, even though we are removed so far from the initial context. The cities of that time were walled for their defense. Watchmen were placed on the wall to survey the horizon for any approaching enemies and were responsible to warn the people of such. When the people were warned, they had an opportunity before the enemy came upon them to retreat to the safety of the city, where the gates would be closed. The city itself would also have opportunity to muster its defense and send for any needed aid. If the watchmen failed, the enemy would overwhelm the citizens who were unprepared and sack the city that was undefended.

That metaphor is applied to the office of the prophet. The prophet is the watchmen. For Ezekiel the enemy is the wrath of God, in this case exercised by the coming armies sent by God to destroy the nation. The citizens are the house of Israel who are continuing in their wickedness without warning. God in His grace provided a prophet, who, as a watchman, sees the coming wrath of the enemy (who is ultimately God), who is given the role of warning the people. He cries aloud and lifts up his voice as a trumpet (Isa 58:1). He shows people their present vulnerability (their wickedness) and calls them to the safety of the city (God's truth).

See then the role of the prophets. They are called on to hear the word that has proceeded from the mouth of God. That is the sufficient source of truth. The prophets declare the reality of sin and judgment. And on the basis of that alone, they are to warn the people who believe themselves to be at safety in their sin and rebellion against their God. How shall they hear without a preacher (Rom 10:14–17)?

However, the metaphor does not function only as a descriptor of the role of a prophet but also as a warning to the prophet. The prophet in the role of watchman may fail. If the watchman fails, it will not change the fate of the wicked. Ignorance of the coming judgment will save no one from that judgment. The tornado comes both on those that heard and did not listen to the warning of the siren, and it comes on those that did not hear the siren at all. They will die in their sins, even if they did not hear the warning from the watchman. God has said to all of mankind, "Dying you will die. . . ." the Hebrew idiom for certainty, or "assuredly you will die." If the one given the task of warning about judgment fails, the judgment, like an invading army still marches forward. Those believing they are safe in their business outside the walls of salvation will indeed meet the opposing sword. Turning a blind eye to the danger, a deaf ear to the sound of the hooves, and holding a mute tongue toward the leisurely wicked is an act of treason against the one that set the watchman in their station and an act of utter hatred against them that are perishing.

The failure to declare the warning of God results in liability on the part of the watchman. James stated that the teacher faces greater condemnation due to their responsibility to speak the truth (James 3:1). God will seek them out in His perfect justice, will bring the watchman into account, and will require him to bear the penalty of his wickedness. The sin here is bloodguilt, to bear the responsibility for the death of another. God said that the death of the wicked who were not warned of the coming judgment is a death for which the one knowing of it and doing nothing to warn is also liable for.

The bloodguilt is apparent in the parallel passage given to Ezekiel. If the watchman sounds the alarm and the wicked ignore it, then they will die for their guilt alone. "Then whosoever heareth the sound of the trumpet, and taketh not warning; if the sword come, and take him away, his blood shall be upon his own head." (Ezek 33:4) The hope is that they will hear the warning and run for refuge. If they do not, they bear the responsibility for themselves. But if they never heard their warning, their guilt for their sin remains, but a new guilt is brought forth; the guilt of the one that allowed the death of one that could have fled for refuge.

The duty of the ministry includes warning the wicked in this world to preach in and out of season, when the message is approved by the populace or when it is hated (II Tim 4:2). The judgment is set, and "as many as have sinned without law, shall also perish without law." (Rom 2:12) Ignorance of the law and its threatening is no excuse to the willful sinner that will not even hear the voice of their own conscience. Conversely, the servant tasked by God to warn the wicked does know what God expects of them. Unlike the sinner, they know that God has commanded them to warn, and the only discharge from this service is its completion. Paul told those at Ephesus, "Therefore watch, and remember, that by the space of three years I ceased not to warn every one night and day with tears. . . ." (Acts 20:31) We cannot say we care for men if we do anything less. The true humanitarian is the one serving the people in regard to their greatest need. We desire to say, like Paul in the same context, "Wherefore I take you to record this day, that I am pure from the blood of all men." (Acts 20:26) It is the preaching of the Gospel that delivers us from such bloodguiltiness.

We cannot set aside the word of God. By it and it alone men are warned (Ps 19:11). We cannot hide this light from them to whom it was given (Matt 5:14–16), nor can we set aside our task of going forward as ambassadors for Christ declaring the need for all to be reconciled to their God (II Cor 5:18–21).

This duty of the Christian watchman is somewhat brought before our minds by Jude. "And others save with fear, pulling them out of the fire; hating even the garment spotted by the flesh." (Jude 1:23) There are some before us that desperately need the warning of God. They are headed into the fire of God's final judgment. They need us to lay the fear of God before them, to snatch them from that fire. God has indeed chosen the foolishness of our preaching to save them that believe (I Cor 1:18). "Knowing therefore the terror of the Lord, we persuade men. . . ." (II Cor 5:11) The message of Hell needs to be declared, for it is a coming danger and we are accountable as God's watchmen to care for our fellow man enough to sound the alarm that they might flee to God for refuge.

PART 2

The Goodness of God

"Behold therefore the goodness and severity of God: on them which fell, severity; but toward thee, goodness. . . ."

ROMANS 11:22

EARLIER THE RIGHTEOUS SEVERITY of God was highlighted. The judgment of God is of necessity severe in its exercise, for it is just. A God that winks at sin is not the holy and righteous God of Scriptures, the Judge of all the earth. The other side of the coin is the goodness of God (Rom 11:22). This goodness, of necessity, has already been seen while the severity of God was proclaimed. However, this goodness now needs to be the singular focus.

Paul spoke of a people who in time were subject to the severe judgment of God due to their disobedience. And in that same context, Paul spoke of a people that had received the grace of God, contrary to their wickedness. God chose to extend to them real salvation through His goodness.

Returning again to our thesis statement, we move from the severity of the first part of the statement to the grace of the second part of the statement:

> "The all-wise, all-good, and just Lord of all has revealed the fearful truth and severity of His justice to be given to sinful men at the end of the age, *but in His love toward the sinner has provided salvation through His Son that the sinner might flee from that wrath to come.*"

As noted, the doctrine of Hell is intended to be a fearfully declared reality, but even in the declaration of its severity, there is grace toward a better end. It is not presented as a fatalistic end that a sadistic God declares to hopeless mankind. God declared judgment and also declared hope. He has turned men to destruction in their sin and has called them to return to Him (Ps 90:3). Hell is that which a loving and merciful God declares, working repentance in the heart of the wicked while simultaneously declaring that there is a refuge where they might flee.

In the backdrop of the declaration of Hell is the God that has made a means that men may escape that wrath. This is done, not by ignoring the justice of God, that underpins our moral reality, but by honoring it. God made a way through Christ that our sins may be righteously judged, yet our sins may be graciously forgiven. It is to that reality we will turn our attention.

We actually may find the good news to be even more offensive than the bad news, for what is the real offense of the doctrine of Hell but the lostness of our nature and our inability to save ourselves? No greater offense can be given than to be told that in our own strength we will fall short. Salvation from Hell is the needed and humbling message that proud men must hear. They must look for salvation from outside of themselves. Hell is the ultimate and final statement of our falling short of the glory of God permanently.

Two brief points need to be addressed in the light of Hell as a doctrinal truth. The love of God has been shown, and the mercy of God has been extended. There is no need for men in that light to be hurt by the second death.

Chapter 8

Despite the Fact of Hell, the Love of God Has Been Shown

"But God commends his love toward us, in that, while we were yet sinners, Christ died for us."

Romans 5:8

Up to this point, I have spoken of death as it is taught biblically, as being separation instead of non-existence. Now, I would like to press further and highlight something about the nature of death which makes its biblical definition more familiar to our natural eyes. This aspect of death is its impassibility. The fearful reality of final judgment, or Hell, is the great gulf that is fixed; the great gulf that makes it impossible for one to pass from one state to another. When Adam died, if it were not for God seeking him, he would have continued to hide from his God. The allegory of death, that is the use of it as a familiar term, is fitting to our understanding. To be physically dead, the life being separated from the body, means that the one who has died is now insensible to the physical world. They cannot hear, move, or respond to anything in this world. Lazarus would have remained dead if Christ, who had authority and power over death, did not call him and raise him from it. The dead know nothing in this world and all their schemes are null and voided (Ecc 9:5). So it is also with those who are spiritually dead in sin. They, too, cannot hear, move, or respond; and they, too, cannot pass from the state of their deadness to life. The dead sinner, separated from the

Living God, cannot come to God unless there is first grace (Eph 2:1–5). The spirit of the unregenerated cannot subject themselves to God (Rom 8:6–8). And Hell, as the second or final death, is equally impassible. It is the final state from which no recovery is possible. Only God can quicken (in the King James language), or give life, to the dead. He is quickening many now from their sins, but the time will come when death is final.

It is this present hope of salvation that is now our focus, for the hope of salvation, the declaration that God is quickening the dead, is now, and not then. Surveying the diverse teachings on Hell, at least those that attempt to affirm it as a reality (i.e., traditional, conditional, and restorational), it is inevitable that they relate to soteriology. After all, we are saved from something, and Hell represents the fulness of that from which we are saved. Even if the existence of Hell is denied, it cannot help to say something about the doctrine of salvation. If there is no Hell, then there is no need of salvation. If Hell is merely an allegory for our fear, education becomes salvation. If Hell is our experience of social pressure, then an act of individual will then become salvation. And on and on the examples could go.

The moral bankruptcy of such views makes the matter of salvation of no real consequence and cannot meet the need of the writer or reader of these sentences. Therefore, we pass on to that which the God who has actually spoken, from whose wrath (i.e., Hell) we need salvation, has said.

Restorationist also offer up a salvation from Hell that saves after Hell is already realized. There is a danger, like all the pagan ideas alluded to shortly above, of shifting salvation in its actuality to some future time. This danger puts all hope in God choosing to raise some from death to life, from Hell to Heaven, after final judgment and not before. Of those possible views that assert the reality of Hell, the most insidious is the restorative view, for it denies the central truths of the Gospel of Christ, the Gospel which alone can save (Rom 1:16, 17). In introduction to our understanding of how the doctrine of Hell relates to the Gospel, a somewhat fuller treatment of this model of Hell is now merited. Anything that denies the Gospel and our need to be saved thereby is an enemy of the word of God. And without the least bit of embarrassment, I declare a conviction that the restorational view of Hell is an enemy of the Gospel of Jesus Christ. Salvation is affected only by the Gospel of Christ (Rom 1:16). I say this not of the conditional view, though I have raised concerns with many of its tenants.[1] One may

---

1. Note: there is a sense in which conditionalism presents annihilation as a kind of salvation from Hell, deeming non-existence to be a better fate, a salvation that occurs as a

be able to hold a conditional view of Hell without denying truths of salvation, but one cannot hold a restorative view without holding a fundamental misunderstanding of the nature of salvation which is alone found in Christ.

On a spectrum with "No Hell" and its absolute denial of Hell as a biblical or sound teaching on the extreme left side of the spectrum and the traditional view (i.e., everlasting conscious suffering—which is defended humbly in this treatise) on the extreme right, the restorative model would be on the left side closer to the "No Hell" position and conditionalism to its right closer to the traditional view. This is a simplistic example, but it will help us visualize the relationship of these views to one another and to the Scriptures themselves. A such, the spectrum would highlight how committed to a faithful and biblically dependent hermeneutic the one that holds their view purports (See figure below). The one who says that there is "No Hell" will deny all clear and certain declarations of the Scriptures in favor of human reasoning. The restorative doctrine will to a lesser extreme do such. As well, the conditional view will still to a lesser degree do such.

Views of Hell

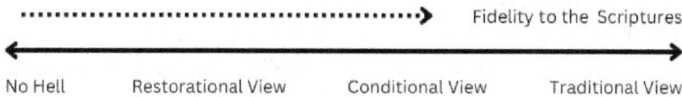

Fidelity to the Scriptures

| No Hell | Restorational View | Conditional View | Traditional View |

I cannot here begin to attempt to offer a full refutation of the restorational view but will rather attempt in a summary way to address its major contentions. The restorative model suffers first from its inability to separate itself from the "No Hell" position, which is intrinsically universalist in its ideology. No one in either scheme ultimately needs salvation in any real sense, for there is nothing ultimately to be saved from. The "No Hell" position offers immediate salvation from Hell by denying its existence and the restorational view offers eventual salvation from Hell after the process of Hell is experienced. The restorative model asserts Hell and salvation as realities but not in the actual sense of those terms. One does not need to be saved in a restorative model, for salvation is not something that comes from outside of the person, destroying the passive notion of deliverance taught in the

---

consequence of our finite destructible natures enduring real fire and not from the Gospel of Christ. But I pass on that depiction and will not here press it.

Scriptures (Lazarus could do nothing unless Christ came to him and gave him life). And Hell is asserted by these false teachers as an unavoidable reality sense the Scriptures mention it but not as a final or eternal reality. Hell as final judgment is not final, and salvation is not something a person needs to receive from a merciful God. These terms cease to have biblical meaning. Salvation from Hell, according to this heresy, will happen automatically by virtue of being sent into Hell, suffering through Hell will save them.

Restorational ideology is much like the traditional Roman Catholic teaching of purgatory. The end, or purpose, of Hell fire is for the purifying or restoration of any that are deemed worthy of its entrance. Like Purgatory, Hell is a process toward something. Those who go to Hell, in the restorative view, do so that they might be saved by enduring their just punishment. The only true difference between restorative ideology and Catholic purgatory is that purgatory for the Catholic traditionally is only for the unsanctified Catholics. However, all people in the restorative model will be restored by suffering in Hell. Hitler, Dahmer, the devil, and his angels will all eventually earn their own salvation and enter heaven. Here, though, there is no final judgment. The great gulf has been removed and all people by a process outside of the Gospel are said to pass from death to life.

Being committed to a view that final judgment is not final, but rather a process of restoration, its adherents lean heavily on biblical language that seems to support universalism and ignore biblical data to the contrary. The reality spoken by Christ that few will find life, many will go into destruction, and that there will be a final dismissal of the wicked is denied (Matt 7:13, 14, 21–23). Contrariwise, when the Scriptures say, "In Christ all shall be made alive. . ." (I Cor 15:22, see also Rom 5:18), it must mean, they say, that everyone will eventually be saved. It cannot take on any other meaning, even if contextually supported. For instance, such texts cannot be about the comparative ends of two separate classes of people (those in Adam and those in Christ). However, such texts in context set forth a difference between what all men naturally have in Adam as sinners under just judgment and what those who have trusted in Christ (all of those) have in Christ.

When Scriptures say that God wills the salvation of all or negatively is not willing that any perish (I Tim 2:4, II Pet 3:9), it must mean, to the restorative advocates, that God has decreed that every person will be saved. They make no difference between the will of God known only to God in His eternal decrees and the imperative will of God expressed to man in His commandments. It is not important that agreement is maintained with the rest of New Testament teachings, nor do other interpretations that mesh with the full revelation (or the immediate context) need to be considered. It cannot mean the elect or all classes of men, in their minds. It cannot mean that God has commanded all to repent.

When it says that Christ is the Savior of all people and the propitiate sacrifice for the sins of the whole world (I John 2:2), to them it cannot mean that Christ claims the exclusive title of Savior, or that salvation must be through Him alone. Instead, universalism is asserted as the only possible meaning. Therefore, all teaching on Hell must be dismissed as only a temporary reality that itself has an end. Any that go there must be ultimately saved according to their doctrine. And without any warrant from any specific teaching on Hell, they believe they have defanged the ultimate fearfulness of the doctrine.

Consider a little closer look at the words of Paul that are often so construed. "[We pray for all men for] it is good and acceptable before God. Who will have all men to be saved, and to come unto the knowledge of the truth." (I Tim 2:1–4) The broader context is here quoted to better bring light to the theological controversy. Indeed, this is speaking about God's will in salvation, and one must tread carefully in order to honor the text and our God. It is God's desire, or will, being expressed. It is expressed towards "all men." If the text is considered at face value, it is a restating of John 3:16. There God loved and here God willed. And the difficulty is the same in both cases. If God wills for all to be saved and all are not saved, does that make God powerless to save? God forbid that we come to such a conclusion regarding the One who is mighty to save (Isa 63:1). We cannot take a position that causes us to deny that our glorious God is able to save (II Tim 1:12, Heb 7:25). The word translated "will" is in the indicative to speak of what is and not in the subjunctive to speak of what might be. There is no conditional factor connected with this proclamation. If any are saved, it is due to God's will. Then if God is able and willing to save, does the text intend to teach that God will indeed save everyone as the restorationists claim? If so, we do not approach the Scriptures as the inherent word of God and we do violence to the agreement of the part to the whole. The Scriptures plainly teach, even Paul elsewhere, that some will be lost. We must respectfully consider this text with greater care.

God is neither powerless nor unjust. If there are many that will be turned away by God, that does not mean that His will to save has been thwarted. In the sense of God's eternal decrees, He does as He wills (Ps

115:3, Isa 46:10). But those hidden decrees belong to Him and His expression of the Gospel belongs to us. To all men therefore, we say, "Come." (II Pet 3:9) "For the grace of God that bringeth salvation hath appeared to all men." (Titus 2:11) Everything about salvation is the will of God expressed. By the will of God Christ was sent, the crucifixion occurred, the Gospel went out, the Spirit convinced, and those that believe were enabled to come. Our God has willed "to save" (in the infinitive, to engage in this act of saving). He is God our Savior, and all our salvation is contingent on Him alone.

This text does not intend to uncover the mystery of election or God's hidden decrees. It only tells us the obvious truth that God has declared (in the "infinitive" as a direct end of what He has done) that He wills "to save" and that among "all men." This is the same "all men" that we are called on to intercede for in ministry in context. He has expressed a will to save without distinction and will have His desire when people of all tongues, tribes, and nations rejoice before Him as a multitude that no man can number. This text is not about God but the minister. The minister is to pray for all men they encounter with the Gospel because God alone is able save all who are saved among them. Asserting salvation from Hell outside of the Gospel after God has exercised final judgment is the height of eisegesis. The broader context of Timothy is that God saves through the means of Christ's mediatorial work alone.

We must take this expression of the will of God in the context in which it is found. We pray and intercede for all men because God has expressed His will to save all men. He sent us to all nations to preach to all kinds of people and told us to pray for them all when we go. In other words, God has not openly expressed to us any limits to His compassion. There are no known limits to the extent of His mercy from our vantage point. He may have mercy on anyone regardless of any boundaries we may think exists. People from every nation, tribe, and tongue will come to know the wonders of this election of God (Rev 5) so we pray for all, knowing and believing that He can save anyone of them and can make the knowledge of Himself known to any. Our Lord is the saving health of all nations (Ps 67:2).

When we see that the election of God is not a detriment to prayer for the salvation of souls, but it is an encouragement to it. The text makes it clear that the choice, or election, of God is the foundation of the salvation of all who come to know it and so the minister intercedes with prayer for all. It is not our will, but His will that saves (John 1:13). The text then conveys this truth, not that God wills to save all men in total, but all men that are saved are saved because God wills to save them. Thus, we pray for all men. Our prayers are meant to come in line with God's expressed will and command for us. He has ordained the means and the end of salvation and desires that we come along His side in the work. Salvation is God's will and a worthy end of our prayers. This will is the expression of the Gospel and now the expression of our intercessions.

Salvation is God's expressed desire to rescue men from sin. If He so wills, they may come to Him freely when He draws them to Him (John 6:44). If they have knowledge of the truth, it is because He has revealed it (John 17:3, 17). If we want to minister the Gospel, we must pray for God to work or else none would be saved. We pray knowing that salvation can only be accomplished by our God, and we intercede now for them before our Sovereign God. If He will have mercy on whomever He wills, we need to pray for mercy to be extended. We do this knowing that in the end, He can harden them in judgment as well (Rom 9:17, 18).

More could be said of this text and others that are used to deny that some will be brought to final judgment. The context of all those texts do not embrace a universalist interpretation. Restorationists, rather, assert that spurious assumption in order to dismiss the finality of Hell. From there, they mount further arguments, not from direct textual teaching on the subject, but from philosophical musings about the nature of God. Just as the "No Hell" position stands on the assertion that God is love, so the restorationists say Hell cannot be a final reality based on the same assertion. The assertion here is that Hell must come from the goodness of God and therefore must be restorative, for a good God must in their mind have only a restorative intent. The further assumption is that the love of God contradicts His expression of justice and goodness when offering direct teaching on the subject of Hell. In their mind, the Scriptures cease to carry infallible authority over their conclusions about God's nature for, they must believe that any language of the Scriptures regarding the finality of judgment must be in error.

What then must be done with direct teaching on Hell? It must be dismissed as hyperbolic or symbolic. Here then is the unfaithful hermeneutic. They say that teaching on Hell is rhetoric that does not describe actual future reality, at least in finality, unless some restorative aspect can be drawn out of it. The only thing that is true about Hell is what they have already decided must be true about Hell, regardless of textual support. It is easy to see at this point that there is little to separate the restorative model with the "No Hell" position.

The only absolutely literal aspect of any teaching on Hell would be the concept of paying the last farthing (Matt 5:26). But here then is the great travesty. The assumption of restorative ideology is that Hell is the mechanism of transformation for the sinner, it is where *they pay for their own sins by enduring their punishment for themselves.* By doing this, they pass from the second death to eternal life. This is the blasphemous idea that one's own suffering, apart from Christ, can be an acceptable propitiation for sins (Rom 3:19–25). Such a doctrine cannot sustain the message of the Scriptures. We cannot justify ourselves at the judgment or through the judgment. There is only one means of us being justified before God. The heresy of restorative ideology is that it denies the need for Christ right now, at this time, and also at that time, as well.

This gets into the heart of the nature of God's love and justice. Hell is the dark background of the reality of God's justice that causes the glory of His love and grace to shine. Hell serves the glory of God's love and the glory of His justice. There is a sense of awe and rejoicing at the judgment of God in the psalms and songs of Scripture that we miss because we are presently unacquainted with the concept of the glory of God's justice. Since we know not the glory of justice, we end up with a cheap understanding of His love.

Paul couched this in these terms, "But God commends his love toward us, in that, while we were yet sinners, Christ died for us." (Rom 5:8) Passing from death to life is only possible via the agency of God. In the context of this Scripture, the great gulf was crossed by the love of God. The main verb here, *sunistémi*, which in the translation provided is rendered as commends, carries the idea of standing with another or being in agreement. Of the possible translations of the word (e.g., demonstrate, show, prove), the word commend probably still carries the idea best. God has literally set up by our side and offered His love to us in a real palatable way.

His love is expressed, to whom? To sinners it is expressed, commended, and offered. To what kind of sinners is it so expressed? Those that are still sinners or are continuing in sin, His love is expressed and set beside them. The context tells us they were completely without strength and unable to help themselves (Rom 5:6). They were dead and unable to avoid the final death. It tells us that there was no redeemable quality to cause this love to be so expressed toward them (Rom 5:7). And it tells us that they were at complete enmity toward God (Rom 5:10). In that state, God's love is expressed to those in the state of death.

And what is this love, and in what manner was it expressed? It is literally "The of Himself love." It comes wholly out of God. It is love that temporally was shown at the time when the utter helplessness of the dead sinner was fully known, when we were without strength in that right time ("in due time. . . . While we were yet sinners. . . . ." Rom 5:6, 8) In essence this love is God's love that is shown out of the darkness of His judgment against sin.

How was it shown? Christ died for the ungodly (Rom 5:6), those who had no reverence or respect or proper fear of God. Those that hated God had the love of God set up by their side, fully expressed and fully offered. "Christ died for us." (Rom 5:8) What happened on that little hill outside of Jerusalem 2,000 years ago was the "Of Himself love" of God expressed and offered to undeserving sinners. Through it, they received the atonement, or rather the reconciliation (Rom 5:10, 11). Christ passed through death to bring them to life. He traversed the impassable great gulf.

Paul states the result of this as it relates to the final judgment. The death of Christ justifies the sinner. Nothing else can, regardless of universalist claims of restorationism. Death is impassable. "Much more then, being now justified by his blood, we shall be saved from wrath through him." (Rom 5:9) It is only those that are now justified by Christ who will be saved from that coming wrath. There is no hope in that time, for the only hope is now.

There are people marked out by the atoning work of Christ who will not come into condemnation (John 5:24, Rom 8:1, Heb 7:25). There are those that will be swallowed up by that coming wrath, being condemned already (John 3:18). But these will not. Here wrath is "the wrath" set aside or specified by use of the Greek article with no other modifier. It is the ultimate and final wrath of God that Scriptures tell us will one day fall on the wicked. It is what we have simply called Hell. The escape from this wrath is not to suffer through it as the restorationists claim but to be saved now by the death of Christ from it before it comes. If you are now justified through faith in what Christ has done on your behalf, you will, as a result, be saved when the wrath, par excellence, comes at the final judgment.

Here we must highlight the means by which sinners may escape the wrath of God. The expressed, the of-Himself, love of God highlights the instrumental means of salvation. The means of salvation is expressed by the instrumental dative in the Greek. We are now justified "by his blood" and that alone will save us when the wrath of final judgment comes. Love bore the judgment. Love shed its own blood to save its object. Love passed the impassable death. This brings us to the point where love and justice kiss and how amazing the expressed love of God is (Ps 85:10).

We are not saved by enduring justice for ourselves but by Christ enduring our just punishment in our stead (II Cor 5:21). Paul gave commentary on this aspect of salvation in many places. He, for instance, spoke to the Colossians about Christ, "Blotting out the handwriting of ordinances that was against us, which was contrary to us, and took it out of the way, nailing it to his cross. . ." (Col 2:14). The understanding of such a text is easy. There were charges rightly made against us. There was a just indictment written to our hurt. Moses wrote that indictment, as did the prophets. We have been tried and convicted and ready to be executed. Instead of our blood being shed for our bloodguiltiness, that just indictment was nailed to the cross of Christ instead. That is where the accusation against any man was hung, above the head of the one bleeding and dying on a cross for their crimes (Matt 27:35–37). Our indictment was transferred to the King of the Jews. He was made to be our sin (II Cor 5:21). Christ died for us. This is the doctrine of penal substitutionary atonement. And this is the truth denied by the restorative model of Hell.

Justice fell on a substitute who stood in the place of the sinner. Paul elsewhere said that this necessary truth of the Gospel which we preach is in full harmony with the Scriptures (I Cor 15:3). The death penalty hung over the firstborn of Egypt, but the house that offered the lamb and placed its blood on its door post were saved by that blood from the wrath (Ex 12:13). The entire sacrificial system showed the need of the substitute. It was the blood that made atonement (Lev 17:11). These were shadows that passed away when the fullness of Christ, the expressed love of God, was shown. Isaiah summed up this substitutionary love:

> "All we like sheep have gone astray; we have turned everyone to his own way; and the LORD hath laid on him the iniquity of us all. . . . and he was numbered with the transgressors; and he bare the sin of many, and made intercession for the transgressors." Isaiah 53:6, 12

The greatest commentary to this expressed and saving love that saves by the blood of Christ is in the third chapter of Romans. There, the guilt of our sin was fully displayed as we stood with our mouths stopped before the judgment of God (Rom 3:18, 19). There before the fearful judgment, the glorious light of the Gospel shines. His justice and His love saved us. We were all under judgment:

"But now the righteousness of God without the law is manifested, being witnessed by the law and the prophets; Even the righteousness of God which is by faith of Jesus Christ unto all and upon all them that believe: for there is no difference: For all have sinned, and come short of the glory of God; Being justified freely by his grace through the redemption that is in Christ Jesus: Whom God hath set forth to be a propitiation through faith in his blood, to declare his righteousness for the remission of sins that are past, through the forbearance of God; To declare, I say, at this time his righteousness: that he might be just, and the justifier of him which believeth in Jesus." Romans 3:21–26

The nature of the justice of God was not set aside to save us. His love took our sins and gave us His righteousness. That alone allowed us, though guilty sinners, to be justified or acquitted before the bar of God's justice. He remains just and justifies the sinner at the same time. The expressed love of God in the death of Christ answered the paradox of our sin and our salvation in the eyes of His holiness.

In the twenty-first verse, the contrary grace is set up in opposition to our guilty state. We were guilty in sin, but another righteousness that alone can acquit us has been revealed. It is apart from the law in that it does not demand perfection of the works of the law which we have failed to do. Cursed are those who continue not in all things that are written in the law to do them, and whoever breaks one law is guilty of all (Gal 3:10, James 2:10). That curse is Hell (Matt 25:47). It is also apart from the law in that it ceased to rely on ordinances that could not perfectly justify any that observed them but must be repeated continuously (Heb 7:19, 10:1–4).

Grace is manifested, rather, by the expectant witness of the law and the prophets. As stated above, the law and prophets looked forward to Christ, His death and resurrection for the sinner, as that which would fulfill all things once and for all. The law and prophets held place and witnessed that something better was coming.

The twenty-second verse tells us that the righteousness which justifies the sinner is God's own righteousness. Again, it was the of-Himself love that was expressed on the cross. It is extended through the faith of Christ (either meaning Christ's faithfulness in performing all things for us or Christ as the object of our faith). It is extended to all, both Jew and Gentile, for they are all equally guilty before God as sinners. Hence the twenty-third verse tells us that all, both Jew and Gentile, sinned and have failed to attain God's glory. They all lack what is needed, therefore they need an alien righteousness, which is now revealed.

The twenty-fourth verse tells us that this justifying righteousness which is revealed now is received as a gift. It is of the free favor of God extended to all who believe in or trust in it. It is based on the redemption, *apolutrósis*, in reference to what Christ accomplished. We were sold under sin, and the price of redemption was fully paid by the death of Christ. The just payment for sin was made.

That redemption is described fully in the twenty-fifth verse that says in its relative clause that Christ was set forth by God as our propitiate sacrifice. God thus loved the world that He gave His only Son to save the believing (John 3:16). He was the sin offering that, when offered, made the sinner acceptable with God. He was in that sense what the law and the prophets witnessed and hoped for. God did not in His long suffering impute the sins of the guilty to them, for all who looked in faith to the sin offering promised by God in the law were accounted righteous (Rom 3:25, II Cor 5:18, 19). He withheld His wrath to pour it instead on the propitiate sin offering. That is what is now revealed in Christ. Our God was satisfied by the death of His Son in the stead of sinners.

Earlier we spoke about the reality of Christ being better than the old covenant. Christ has come and has accomplished "something" in time and, as a result, "some things" are now different. The difference is the universal application of righteousness of God to all who believe in Christ. The theological question faced by us is, "What are the things that are now different in the light of the fact that Christ has come and finished His work and made the love of God manifest to us?" The ordinances of the law that were written against us were exchanged for the reality of Christ taking their fullness upon Himself. The old covenant offered constant reminders of our guilt in its ordinances. We were constantly in danger of touching some unclean thing and becoming unholy and guilty before our God. But Christ made all things new (II Cor 5:17). There is no more a reminder of wrath and uncleanness set before us in the revelation of Christ. The shadows have passed for the brightness of the Sun. The love of God in Christ removed the fear of wrath and fulfilled all things. The blood of Christ has made us clean, removed our guilt, and we turn not again to the shadows and pictures to be reconciled. God has thus shown us His love. Anyone who will now believe in His atoning death alone is promised that they will not perish. We are saved from the wrath if by the blood of Christ we now stand justified.

Chapter 9

Despite the Justice of Hell, the Mercy of God Has Been Proclaimed

"Verily, verily, I say unto you, He that heareth my word, and believeth on him that sent me, hath everlasting life, and shall not come into condemnation; but is passed from death unto life."

JOHN 5:24

ONE IMPORTANT ADDENDUM STILL needs to be said. Christ died and rose again to die no more (Rom 6:9). Not only did Christ pass over the impassable great gulf to save us, but He also brought us with Him. He that descended has also now ascended (Eph 4:10). He has sat down at the right hand of power (Heb 1:1–3), and all enemies will soon be put under His feet (Ps 110). We have sat down with Him (Eph 2:6, 7). Justification, which was highlighted in the previous chapter, is related to regeneration and leads infallibly to glorification (Rom 8:28–30). Christ quickened us, or raised us from death, by His death and His now glorified life (Heb 7:25). We now will never be condemned, for we have now passed from death to life.

All of this is what Christ does for the one that hears and believes in Him. It is impossible for the dead to participate in their resurrection. The Armenian contention that the dead *can* hear and believe is a fundamental misunderstanding of the term, the reality of the great gulf. There is a complete inability in the sinner (John 6:44). The dead *cannot* do anything. Christ can cause the dead to hear and believe, and thus to come to Him in faith. Again, Lazarus was not able to come out of the grave until Christ came and commanded it. Raising the dead to die no more is what God alone can do. But this raises a new set of objections. Why are some raised to life and faith in Christ and others remain dead to die again in Hell?

One of the most strident objections to the existence of Hell must here be addressed directly as this subject is brought to a close. "How is it fair that God has created some people knowing that they will end in Hell?" That is the formula of the objection often levied by those who hold to libertarian free will, which is not the view of liberty underlying this treatise. Much more needs to be said in regards to libertarianism than can be said in this work, however this discussion will be limited to that which relates to this stringent objection to God's final judgment.

The libertarians would say that God is not the cause of the damnation of any, but one's own libertarian free will is what damns each individual. They imagine reality to be God trying to save everyone but being unable to do so due to the freedom of man. They, contrary to the clear teaching of the Scriptures, lay salvation solely in the will of the creature, on whoever wills (Rev 22:17). The most ardent Calvinist (like me) would not deny that "whosoever will" is the general call that is preached, that salvation is declared in all places, but they do so while knowing that the will of man cannot save any. The dead are separated from God, dead to Him and unable to give themselves life.

There is more to this matter of salvation than the will of man. We are not saved by our will, though we are not saved contrary to our will. "Thy people shall be willing in the day of thy power." (Ps 110:3) God's will is the chief cause of salvation. "[The believing] were born, not of blood, nor of the will of the flesh, nor of the will of man, but of God." (John 1:13) He will show mercy to whom He wills to show it (Rom 9:16). As such, the free will argument fails to answer this matter in a wholly biblical manner. If free will shows anything it is the truth of the hardness of the unrepentant heart of the sinner against God. Man by his own will is not good and does not seek God (Rom 3:10–18). Man's will, as Edwards stated in his work *The Freedom of the Will*, naturally always chooses his chief desire which is sin and not God.

Further, libertarianism fails to answer the objection, for they still have God freely creating creatures that He knows, according to their view of freedom, will not "will to be saved" and will end up in Hell. This is the folly of ideas like Molinism.[1] Some may wish to move further from such

1. Molinism is the belief that God chose out of many possible worlds which world to

a position and adopt an unscriptural and blasphemous view of God that says that God does not know what will be in the future, as the heresies of Open Theism and Process Theology maintains. All the libertarian does in their theology is reduce God to a helpless spectator in the theater of man's drama, unable to fully save any and uninvolved or passive in the judgment of any. Tragically, they open the door to a denial that God does not know what free men will do and is limited in His knowledge. Such is a blasphemous thought and rightly provokes our indignation. He knows all, for He created all and has determined their ends. Salvation and judgment are both exercises of His sovereign power. He saves whomever He wills to save and reserves to judgment and will actually judge whom He wills.

This small work is unable to address the full spectrum of biblical teaching on human freedom without distraction from the topic at hand. However, limited commentary is necessary. The ability of man that is taught in the Scriptures for which man is accountable to God and liable before Him in judgment can be summed up as follows:

What the individual can do:

- One can choose to love or hate their neighbor, to honor or blaspheme God's name, to be kind or cruel to others, to give instead of steal, to be truthful instead of bearing false witness, etc.

- For all of this they will stand before their God one day and give an account, and all of us in a greater or lesser way have real guilt from this perspective. In this liberty, we are all utterly lost and guilty before God.

That which one as a guilty and lost person cannot do:

- They cannot please God (Heb 11:6).

- They cannot as a sinner reconcile themselves to God (John 6:44, 14:6).

- And, therefore, without the faith of Christ, they never can be saved.

- Salvation or deliverance from this sinful state is utterly dependent upon God.

---

actually create (worlds that are created by all possible free will choices made by man and therefore worlds not created by God; middle knowledge not ontologically true because God made it so).

The objection that God is unfair to create people knowing that they will end in Hell must be answered with the reality presented to us in the Scriptures. God's will is the first cause of the salvation of any who believe. The will of the individual is not the cause of salvation, but rather a corresponding truth. The will of man does not contradict salvation or final judgment.

The objection then might rather be recounted like this, if God predestined the end of the saved and the damned, how can He yet judge them? Now, we have already addressed what makes all men guilty before God and worthy of judgment. As has been stated by many, the wonder is not that God chooses to save some, but that He wills to save any. There is nothing redeemable in any of us. He is right to judge and good to save as He pleases. We cannot say to God that He had no right to create us or that He has no right to judge us. The potter has power over the clay. God created all men for His glory. In their own wisdom and freedom, they chose to not retain the knowledge of Him (Rom 1:28). God is glorified in their judgment just as He is in the salvation of some. Our great God created a reality in which both His justice and mercy are glorified.

Predestination is not the same as fatalism, though it is often accused to be such. The history of mankind begins with a sinless man who could have chosen to not sin or rebel against God. That decision was made by Adam on behalf of all men. Now, man does have liberty to act and does within the sovereign rule of God even though he is a sinner. In the image of God in which all are created, the individual may choose between certain things. In that liberty, all men choose sin which is their chief desire. They are lost and dead in sins in that reality, worthy of final judgment. But God chose those that are saved from out of that mass of dead humanity before the creation of the world. Thus, God has elected to save, and by consequence has reprobated the rest, or left them in their unjust and sinful condition.

The question is further complicated. In that reality, has mercy actually been extended to those who by the election of God are left in their lost condition? This seems to be the heart of the matter, for it questions whether mercy is really mercy. The objection is regarding the concept of opportunity or ability to respond. If one has no ability to respond to the mercy of God extended, it is claimed that God is not really merciful.

This objection was met with by Paul by his detractors. When expounding on the will of God in salvation the objection was made, "Why doth [God] yet find fault? For who hath resisted his will?" (Rom 9:19) Paul's answer in that context (see the rest of the chapter) is somewhat enigmatic and leans even more into the Sovereignty of God. God is the potter, and we are but the clay. It is wholly in His power and authority to make of all of us as He pleases. And yet, you who make this foolish objection stand up and contradict and express hostility (*antapokrinomai*) against the absolute ruler. You cannot even make such an objection without proving your resistance toward God. You show that your heart is hard against God, and He as the potter is right to reject you.

Even here the semblance of opportunity is set forth. You had the power to make such a contradiction. Pharaoh was sent a word and with his own will answered instead, "Who is the Lord, that I should hear Him?" If you truly believed that God's will saves, that He will have mercy on whom He wills to show mercy, why are you not falling before Him in humility, crying out for His mercy? You have examples of those who have done so and received mercy. God did not cause you to speak against Him. That lied within your creaturely freedom. Your love of sin chose to contradict God and speak against Him (John 3:19, 20). It was not against your will to answer the Lord in your hardness. The wicked and unfaithful servant who believed that his master's heart was hard still had the opportunity to do right with what was in his power to do. Instead, that wicked servant chose not to honor his lord in any way and accuse him rather of being the reason for his failure (Matt 25:24–27). Your opportunity is apparent. The light of nature was seen. The light of God's law was seen. The light of Christ was seen. How have you responded thus far?

The doctrines of election and reprobation have always been taught as two sides of the same coin of sovereignty. God has a right to do as He pleases or wills. If we are saved it is chiefly because He has chosen based on His own good pleasure to be merciful. If we are damned, it is because He in holiness has chosen to show His wrath against our deserving hardness. This is a God to be rightly feared. The early men of the Reformation would teach that in election God is Sovereign and gracious; in reprobation God is Sovereign and just. He is the one showing His rule in both.

Reality teaches us that salvation and judgment are not impersonal matters, and they ask us to see ourselves before a real, personal, and fearful God who can choose to save or damn. Fear that God. Respond as such. We know nothing about how the eternal God relates temporally to time. What choices He freely made, from our perspective, before creating is beyond our comprehension, but what He reveals to us in time is apparent. The

Syrophoenician woman was told that she was outside of grace, a dog, but that did not keep her from crying for mercy and finding it (Matt 15:26–28). No one who has not cried out earnestly to God for mercy through Christ is able to complain about the nature and extension of God's mercy.

We could not even begin to count the mercies extended that we should and could respond to. There are so many examples given to us in the Scriptures of mercy extended by God and received and mercy extended by God and rejected. The excuse that one has no opportunity to respond is just that, an excuse by one that does not want to respond to God and demands that God be gracious anyway. This is about your response to what is in your power. The foolishness of trying to say to the Creator that He can only create what you in your puny wisdom deemed He should create is the height of hubris. He created as He wills and saves as He wills, and that truth should cause you to fear. Any hardness you have has shown your liability to His final judgment.

The relationship between the Sovereignty of God in election and human responsibility includes a view of liberty that includes man's accountability to God and liability before His judgment. As John Frame in his *Systematic Theology* has pointed out, this all happens not only in the context of His Sovereign control over His creation but also in the real context of His declared law/word authority and covenant Lordship presence with His creatures. He is not just the author of reality but has written Himself into its text. He maintains a righteous, holy, and merciful presence while in His goodness leading the guilty into repentance. Those that are guilty are so in the whole context of the present and fearful God.

The sovereign rule of God encompasses human freedom and thus, it encompasses real human guilt. God determined before the foundation of the world that man would freely sin with real liability and guilt before Him, and He works out His own will in that context. He determined that wicked men would kill the Son and that they would do so knowing that He was their Lord (Acts 2:23). The fact that God decreed the actions of Judas did not change the reality that Judas betrayed Christ with a lie and also with a kiss having been warned that he was betraying the one sent from God (Matt 26:24, 25, 49).

Hell is the product of real judgment. In the end, God has real reason or cause to bring final judgment. When Christ was brought before Pilate, Pilate could find no reason or cause (*aitian*) of death in Him (Luke 23:18–25), but the day will come when we all stand in front of the Judge that knows all we have done. We should be honest enough right now to say He will find sufficient cause to judge us. Final judgment is focusing on real accountability and liability before God. They knew God and they refused Him. They would not in this world with the light given to them respond and submit to God's declared will.

The doctrine of God's Sovereignty is broader than predestination. It declares to the guilty that the will of God will be done. Every knee will bow. In the end, His will is Sovereign, and even the most rebellious will be brought under it. Unfortunately, their obedience to His will one day will be manifest by the command, "Depart from me." Their will on that day will be seen for its inefficacy. They will desire to be saved, but will be told that God will not save them.

The imperative over us is to submit to the will of God now:

> "Strive to enter in at the strait gate: for many, I say unto you, will seek to enter in, and shall not be able. When once the master of the house is risen up, and hath shut to the door, and ye begin to stand without, and to knock at the door, saying, Lord, Lord, open unto us; and he shall answer and say unto you, I know you not whence ye are: Then shall ye begin to say, We have eaten and drunk in thy presence, and thou hast taught in our streets. But he shall say, I tell you, I know you not whence ye are; depart from me, all ye workers of iniquity." Luke 13:24–27

The disobedience of man will not stand as an unjudged reality. Today, if you hear His voice, do not be obstinate against His will as it is declared, for the day will come where you must do His will. His merciful hand is now extended but will not be so forever. The warning of God to obstinate Judah rings true still:

> "But they refused to hearken, and pulled away the shoulder, and stopped their ears, that they should not hear. Yea, they made their hearts as an adamant stone, lest they should hear the law, and the words which the Lord of hosts hath sent in his spirit by the former prophets: therefore came a great wrath from the Lord of hosts. Therefore it is come to pass, that as he cried, and they would not hear; so they cried, and I would not hear, saith the Lord of hosts." Zechariah 7:11–13

The sentence of death hangs over the guilty man. The grave is their transition to that reality. They will pass from the first death to the second. The rich man was buried and then opened his eyes in the state of that death.

He was there in torment and was also reminded that in this life there was real mercy extended. Even though he claimed it to be insufficient, in his ignorance he was told that those of his kindred had Moses and the prophets (Luke 16:29). No one is without mercy extended from God. The revelation of God has been heard in every language (Ps 19:1–6). The Gospel has gone forward to every nation with the message of repentance and remission of sins (Luke 24:47). Those who reject the will of God today do so with even greater light and mercy extended to them than the rich man would have ever known.

In the context of the reprobation of the lost stands the glorious truth of God's electing mercy, His choice to have mercy on some. Mankind as a whole is guilty and under that sentence of death. But God chose to save some in Christ (Eph 1:4–6). The Book of Life is that allegory of the electing love and covenant mercies of God who chose to save those who are written therein. Jesus told His disciples to rejoice in that electing love, that their names are written in heaven (Luke 10:20). As the high priest bore the names of the children of Israel on their breastplate and shoulders, so Christ bore the names of all who would be saved by His work. Thus, His death and resurrection actually saved the elect.

The Book of Life will be opened at the final judgment. After showing the wicked that they deserve their fate, it will also be shown that they are outside of any electing mercy. That mercy they despised will be seen to have no part for them. Their names will not then be found in that Book which was written before the foundation of the world (Rev 13:8, 20:11–15). It is called the Lamb's Book, for it contains those that were His to save by His death and endless life (Heb 7:25). What we know about these elect people is that in time they come to Christ (John 6:37). They have the promise that their names will never be blotted out of the book of life (Rev 3:5). And they belong to the same class of people that will never be hurt by the second death (Rev 2:11, I John 5:4, 5). Christ said that it is these same objects of electing mercy that live and believe in Him, and they will never die (John 11:25, 26). They are unlike the wicked who will in the final judgment be given over to the second and final death (Rev 20:15).

This mercy now extended is central to the Gospel message. It goes forth with the merciful declaration that, though we are all rightly condemned, we through faith in Christ can be delivered. He died our death for us, and we live now only in Him. There is great assurance here for any that will receive Him. "Verily, verily, I say unto you, He that heareth my word, and believeth on him that sent me, hath everlasting life, and shall not come into condemnation; but is passed from death unto life." (John 5:24) The final judgment of Hell, in the end, will be for all who refused to hearken and would not trust the record or message God declared (I John 5:6–13). It is not that the merciful God did not speak. It is that man despised His voice and went their own way.

Appendix:
The Meaning of Suffering

"By faith Moses, when he was come to years, refused to be called the son of Pharaoh's daughter; Choosing rather to suffer affliction with the people of God, than to enjoy the pleasures of sin for a season; Esteeming the reproach of Christ greater riches than the treasures in Egypt: for he had respect unto the recompence of the reward. By faith he forsook Egypt, not fearing the wrath of the king: for he endured, as seeing him who is invisible."

Hebrews 11:24–27

WHILE DISCUSSING HELL, WE were forced to give some attention to the reality of suffering and its relationship to the so-called Problem of Evil, an argument used by anti-theist to deny the reality of the God of the Scriptures. Being unable in the body of the treatise on Hell to give a more careful treatment to the truth of suffering, a brief declaration is rendered here. While this will not answer all questions about suffering, it will hopefully lay the groundwork for further study.

The issue ultimately concerning suffering is regarding the question of its meaning. This may seem like a subjective aspect, but as we will see suffering is a subjective phenomenon. Meaningless suffering is the only truly horrifying thought. Meaningful suffering is easier to fathom, cope with, and endure. Everyone, when they suffer, will ask the inevitable question "Why!" demonstrating that everyone believes suffering has meaning and significance even when we presently do not know what it is. The most ardent nihilist will ask why such a thing is happening when enduring the pangs of misery. It is assumed by all, though often unspokenly so, that what we go through is not by random chance. We all know the God of the Scriptures exists, who works all things according to His good pleasure (Ephesians 1:1–14). If suffering has meaning, and it most certainly does, it becomes bearable and even meaningful.

The true hideousness of Hell is the end of existential meaning for suffering. It will have ontological meaning for the glory of God and moral meaning as a symbol of Justice, but no possibility of existential good for the one under it. Those that are in it will not have any purpose. It will not be to a greater end for them, and therefore only serves as their eternal and just penalty. Hell is the vanity of vanities. That is an end to be feared. Hell is where the termination line of all possible good for suffering is drawn. Hell is the worst of all possible realities reserved for rebellious sinners. Anything we have to say about present suffering is immediately part of a better context.

There is no need to defend the merited end of suffering in Hell unless man wishes to deny their guilt and liability before God. The question of suffering then turns to reality as we now know it. The argument against Biblical theism on the basis of suffering is not scientific or intellectual in nature. It is not fought in the arena of objective truth but subjective feelings. It is rather existential and emotional in nature. It is often couched as if it was a purely intellectual conclusion, but in reality, is solely emoted. Consider a popular syllogism:[1]

- If God is all-powerful, then God could create a world in which suffering does not exist.

- If God is all-good, He would do so.

- Therefore, God is either not all-good or He is not all-powerful.

- Since the Bible says God is all-good and all-powerful, the God of the Bible does not exist.

This line of reasoning is admittedly powerful, because it touches us on an emotional level. We feel the argument and therefore rarely question its validity. Any intellectual arguments about why suffering exists are seemingly meaningless to the person who is actually touched by suffering. When touched by suffering, intellectual truisms give little comfort. One cannot

1. A slightly different formula is used from the earlier formula in order to offer a stronger wording against my present argument.

seem to escape and we are likely to cry out as did Solomon in his Ecclesiastes, "All was vanity." (Ecc 1:2)

The Book of Job addresses the question of the righteous person suffering. We as readers have the benefit of seeing the heavenly backdrop and context to all that Job was experiencing. Spiritual warfare was being engaged that Job was not aware of, which created the backdrop for his suffering. However, Job never got answers as to the reason for his suffering, at least no answers were recorded. The book unfolds with an intellectual conversation between Job and his friends about the cause of Job's misery. God rebuked all for darkening His counsel without knowledge (Job 38:2). When God finally spoke, He did not offer Job any answers. Instead, God asked Job a long series of questions designed to show Job the greatness of God above all. The answer to suffering for the Christian then is found in the substance of their faith; in the greatness of the God that they worship. They see God as worthy of their worship and just in His dealings with them, ultimately rewarding them for their sufferings.

The Biblical answer to suffering lies in the nature of God. As we experience a neopagan revival, the meaning of suffering is lost. There are many energies and gods at work but no one true God overall and therefore, there can be no ultimate reason why. It is all arbitrary in the pagan world. If the God of the Scriptures does not exist, there is no reason to seek a universal understanding of individual suffering as feigned by those who use the Problem of Evil syllogism. There would be no ultimate reason for whatever is happening.

Approaching the reality of present suffering from the secular and agnostic position, the position of the above syllogism, cuts off the sufferer from viewing suffering through the eyes of faith. There is no rational warrant in approaching the problem of suffering as such on an intellectual level. Secularism will not allow for meaning from the start, it already assumes that there can be no meaning other than it just happens.

Passing over those observations, the intellectual side of the Problem of Evil argument is actually quite anemic. It is built upon faulty premises, which create a false dilemma. It assumes that there is no other attribute of God that is applicable to our understanding of suffering, such as God being all-wise. Could an all-wise, all-good, and all-powerful God have good reason to allow for suffering in this world? The answer is obviously yes. A doctor has a reason to use a scalpel or reset a broken leg. An all-wise God may indeed, and most certainly does, have higher wisdom and knowledge than is in the objector. However, the objector in the syllogism themselves claim to be all-wise to know that God could not have a higher reason. They deny God something they assume for themselves.

That is not the only rational hurdle for the syllogism. It assumes the existence of logic (hence the syllogism) and an objectively meaningful moral reality (i.e., it is not good for God to allow suffering). It is incoherent from an agnostic view to believe that reality is logical or moral. God is necessary for a logical and moral reality. But the syllogism denies God.

Also, the argument could easily be flipped and be just as valid. If God does not exist because of all the evil and suffering that exists, then how is the existence of good and delightful things accounted for? We, after all, live in a world where both taste buds, spices, and sweets exist. What a wonderful world indeed!

And what of the influence of agency outside of God? The Scriptures answer the existence of natural evil as being a result of moral evil. Suffering is the result of judgment against sin, and the sinfulness of men is an aggravating factor in much, rather all, of the ongoing suffering experienced in this world. God uses such suffering to work greater ends (Rom 8:28), but moral responsibility for evil and its consequences lies at the feet of men. The objector and their syllogism ignore this feature of suffering and attempt to claim divine culpability. It is common knowledge that the looters, thieves, and corrupt men cause more suffering after the natural disaster than the natural disaster itself. Human agency is usually an aggravating factor to painful events. Job did not wish to die until his friends first spoke.

Underlying the syllogism, as a whole, there is the assumption that an all-good God must create the best-of-all-possible worlds first (i.e., A world without the possibility of suffering). God is just as righteous if this present world is probationary in nature prior to a permanent world where suffering and sin will not be. In fact, God would be just as righteous to have not created a world at all or to have judged the world immediately and permanently after the fall. What is unrighteous is for the creature to demand of the Creator that He must create the world in such and such a fashion or that He must not first judge them in a probationary reality. They want the best of all possible worlds without having to submit to the Lordship of God or seek His will first. They desire a heaven without God, all while relying on God to create it for them.

Ultimately, the revelation of God offers an answer for the Problem of Evil or suffering that leaves the syllogism empty and vacuous. God has not only allowed and decreed in His justice that suffering exists in this world but has Himself entered that suffering in order to redeem it. The Scriptures do not present a God of indifference, but a Savior that is acquainted with all points of our suffering. Christ "suffered once," but has through His suffering brought complete salvation from the reality of sin. Suffering is for a short time and has its termination at the resurrection of Christ. Those that are His will awake unto righteousness one day where all tears are wiped away. In the face of the resurrection, the reality of suffering loses all of its horror and replaces it with a world of hope.

These intellectual and theological answers do not in and of themselves declare meaning to particular points of suffering, but they demonstrate that, due to the nature and work of our God, suffering is not without present meaning and value. We call suffering evil because it is the product of evil, the product of the immoral choices of man, the righteous judgment upon them, and the judgment of the world as man is the representative head of creation. But suffering is not evil in any moral sense.

We live in a world where evil happens. There are two kinds of evil occurrences that bring about suffering. There is natural evil, such as disease or natural disaster. Then, there is volitional evil, which is the product of moral choices and the consequences thereof. We have all been touched with these kinds of evil and have faith, as Christians, that there will one day be an end to them through Christ. Yet we do suffer them and desire above all things to find meaning in them. That is, again, why the natural response to suffering is to ask the question "Why?"

Only if suffering was void of all meaning in this life could the syllogism carry any existential weight. But there is no meaningless life and there is no meaningless experience in life. This is the real weakness for the Problem of Evil argument, for if there is no God then the syllogism leaves those that believe its conclusion with a present world of meaningless suffering.

To the Christian, the world of suffering finds its greatest meaning in the expression of faith. Faith of any sort may give a semblance of meaning, but only faith in the truth of God can provide true meaning. Victor Frankl rightly pointed out that it was faith and a sense of purpose that enabled men to survive the death camps of Nazi Germany.[2] Faith gives meaning to people enduring suffering, and therefore, the syllogism does nothing to answer the problem of suffering. Its voice is a voice against resilience. It leaves us with a reality more like the movie *They Shoot Horses, Don't They*,

2. Frankl, Victor; *Man's Search for Meaning*.

where Depression-era contestants dance in a marathon in hunger for a meaningless prize.

To the contrary, the eleventh chapter of Hebrews deals with how faith acts in the reality in which we live; how it presses forward despite opposition and suffering. To the believer, the faith of Christ is an active element. By faith Enoch offered, by faith Abraham went out and obeyed. By faith Sarah received strength. By faith Abraham offered. By faith Jacob worshiped. And by faith the parents of Moses hid the baby because they feared not the king. These men and women believed, trusted, and obeyed their God through suffering for the glory of their God. Their suffering had meaning. The end of the chapter speaks of faith doing great acts and faith enduring intense suffering at the hands of the wicked world. Faith without works is not real faith. Faith without works is dead. It is not faith at all. Faith acts in a reality of suffering and pain. There is no other way in which it may be expressed.

Moses, as a case study in that chapter, was born a Hebrew and born at a time when Hebrew baby boys were being exterminated. He was born to godly parents who kept him alive despite the command to kill him. However, when he could no longer be hidden, they committed him to the Nile River where Pharaoh's daughter discovered him. She took him unto herself and raised him as her own child. He grew up in Egypt and was taught with all of the wisdom of Egypt. He could have had all the treasures of Egypt and enjoyed all of its pleasures. Nevertheless, the text says this: "By faith Moses, when he was come to years, refused to be called the son of Pharaoh's daughter . . . ."

Moses refused Egypt. This was a decision that was done by faith. That means that he heard the word of God and believed it and acted on it. It was not presumption that caused Moses to refuse all the possibilities of Egypt. He refused Egypt because he believed God about the promises of Israel and he embraced those promises. He did not make this decision rashly either, but did so when he had come of age. He refused Egypt and chose something else. He chose suffering.

Moses is a man that "chose to suffer" instead of having those pleasurable and comfortable things in Egypt. He found meaning in it. Why would any person choose a life of suffering when they could have the riches, ease, comforts, and pleasures of the world? The text explains why Moses did these things and challenges us to choose such a life of suffering, as well. The pattern of Moses is seen more fully in Christ as well, "Wherefore, Jesus also, that he might sanctify the people with his own blood, suffered without the gate. Let us go forth, therefore, unto him without the camp, bearing his reproach. For here have we no continuing city, but we seek one to come." (Heb. 13:12–14)

Christianity is not interested in escaping the cross but in embracing and carrying the cross. It calls for great acts of faith. The history of Christianity is a glorious story of suffering after the pattern of its Lord. Suffering that turned the world upside down. The apostles gladly suffered, and therefore thousands were converted. The martyrs gladly embraced the lions and the stake. Moreover, through their martyrdom, the world has seen the beauty of the faith of Christ. Christianity is a story of enduring suffering and not escaping it; enduring it for the sake of a greater end that is not necessarily futuristic in nature but immediately valuable.

The Christian does not deny the existence of suffering. Buddhism and other eastern religions deny its existence, but not the Christian. The Christian embraces suffering, not as a Stoic without feeling but by the expression of their faith. They proclaim that there is a greater meaning to it, as well as a belief that one day all will be set right. This stands in great contrast to the empty view of atheism, which at best is a defiant form of defeatism that says there is no meaning to the things that we suffer and that there is no greater purpose. The Christian believes there is a present meaning for the things that they suffer, and it is for that reason that they have courage to take up their cross.

In doing so, Christianity has become a force for relieving the suffering of many in this world. It has a declared theology of suffering. One that declares real meaning to the emotional question that suffering brings with it. There is a reason. The very thing that the Problem of Evil syllogism argues against is the strength of the Christian perspective. When Job sat in ashes and proclaimed that God was to be praised, that reason was fulfilled. Faith in the truth of God expressed through suffering answers the question of meaning; the why that we long to know.

What is the nature of suffering? Suffering is different from pain. Both pain and suffering entered the world through sin. We often intertwine the two and believe them to be the same, and often they can be used interchangeably in or daily language. Pain is something that happens to someone; an injury of various natures. There is physical pain, psychological, and emotional pain. And there is spiritual pain. Pain is an event that happens or continues to happen to a person or to a group of people. Suffering is not an event that happens to a person. It is something that a person chooses to do. To suffer means to bear what is painful or to endure. To sink under a weight. It is synonymous with the words patience and endurance.

It is, no doubt, puzzling to hear suffering described as a choice. Who would ever choose suffering? An example of this may be a person choosing suffering by refusing to take pain medication. A more exact example may be found in the world of literature and storytelling. Every great story has an element of suffering in it; we often call it the conflict of the story. The hero of the story at some point decides to suffer through something or to endure something for the sake of gaining something else. The warrior chooses suffering over cowardice. The body builder chooses suffering or enduring the pain of exercise in order to gain physical fitness. Sometimes we hear about the cancer patient choosing to suffer pain in order to maintain their consciousness and wits. They would do this because they desire not to be in a comatose state when their loved ones are by their side. Suffering is what a person, or a group of people, decides to do with their pain. Suffering is the result of freedom, or rather it is an expression of freedom or liberty, upholding human dignity and not disparaging it. The one that suffers does so in liberty.

Pain is a great thing because it tells us when something is wrong. Suffering is a great thing because it creates opportunities. Because we live in a world of suffering, we live in a world where accomplishments could be made by the grace of God. Without suffering, words like love, forgiveness, and honor would have no real meaning. There would be no examples of great lovers and great heroes. It is worth it to endure suffering for the right things. That is why James told us that we count them happy that endure (James 5:11).

Every time a painful event occurs, a decision is to be made by the one that sustains that injury. What am I going to do with my pain? Am I going to try to escape the pain or am I going to choose to patiently endure the pain? The painful event puts a fork into the road and makes us choose; escape or suffering. The choice to escape pain takes many forms in culture: drugs, alcohol, sensual relationships, entertainment (which is a diversion), work, play, etc. While escape is not always a bad thing, it is a terrible thing if there is never a choice to suffer, especially for the glory of God.

This is the essence of the choice. Painful events are testing and reveal what we truly are. We are what we really are when the pressures of life reveal it. What does it take for you to stop doing what is right? Would it take thirty pieces of silver or a moment of sinful pleasure? Some base the whole of their happiness upon avoiding or escaping pain. They are constantly seeking diversion, and therefore never live for any higher purpose than their own happiness. However, they are not happy in their life of diversion. Pascal once pointed out that if people were truly happy, then the less they were diverted the happier they would be.[3] The fact that we have to constantly try to divert ourselves is a clear sign that escape does not make us happy. Our culture wants to be entertained everywhere: home, church, work, etc. Yet our culture is chronically depressed! True joy can only come when we endure for a higher purpose.

Moses showed a set of three dialectics in his choice to suffer that are worth pondering in a brief case study: people against pleasures (v. 25), testimony against treasures (v. 26), and the sight of God against the strength of the king (v. 27). In each dialectic a choice is presented. Will one choose to suffer for the greater principle or will they choose to escape from it to the lesser and baser principle. The pleasures of sin for a season are an escape. The treasures of Egypt are an escape. The fear of the king is an escape. This is true especially when God has revealed a greater end through suffering that calls us to forsake these things. Too often people see no value to suffering, and therefore they despise the cross.

Unfortunately, the church also now sees no value in suffering and holds little or no place for it in their theology. There is now no place for the cross in the church, where every message is therapeutic, and every promise seems to be for self-centered prosperity. As has been said by many, we want Christianity without a cross, a Gospel without sin, and preaching without guilt or conviction. The average Christian sinks into their various forms of escape: sin, diversion, or compliance with the present evil world. We see no value in enduring the pain of standing up for people, living for Christ, or seeking God. We are convinced, along with the world, that suffering is a bad thing to be avoided at all costs, and therefore we refuse to suffer because we see no present or eternal value in it. Unlike Job, we do not see suffering as the means by which we may come forth as gold; purer, truer, and better suited for service and glory. Therefore, when pain comes, we choose to escape.

The ethics of the unbelieving world is to escape suffering. Therefore, the moral philosophies of the world leave no room for faith, much less love and bravery and honor. Why should we be willing to choose suffering? We should be willing to choose it because there is something more valuable

3. Pascal, Blaise, *Pensées*.

than our personal ease or comfort. Until we grasp this, we will never carry the cross that Christ has asked us to carry. Moses saw the value of these things, and therefore he chose to suffer.

Moses saw *people as greater than pleasures*. Moses chose "rather to suffer affliction with the people of God, than to enjoy the pleasures of sin for a season . . . ." He saw the best this world has to offer and weighed it against the value of the people he cared for, the people belonging to God. He found the latter to be of greater weight. Here then is the fork in the road. The way of suffering is connected with the decision to stand up with and for others, specifically the people of God. The way of escape is to live a life of sinful pleasure for yourself. The easiest thing in the world for any individual to do is to live a life of sin, for the pleasures of sin pull on the most selfish and natural strings within us. It appeals to all we desire in our fallenness.

However, only one of these choices can have lasting benefits. Matthew Henry stated in commentary of this text that sinful pleasure must end in repentance or ruin, and that soon.[4] It is only a seasonal thing before it leaves one empty. Sin at its core is self-centered and self-absorbed. Unless we see meaning in the pain of service toward the people God gave us as being of greater value than escape, escape will always seem to be the most attractive and reasonable response, even at the expense of others.

Sinful pleasure pushes everyone underneath the pursuer of that pleasure. The drug addict will steal from those they love to find their escape. The drunkard will not care about those that are close to them who they are hurting or putting at risk. The sexually immoral person will not care about the feelings they are hurting, the homes they are wrecking, or the futures they are ruining. Sin at its core is selfish. Sin despises suffering and chooses selfishness. But it will never lead to a life of fulfillment.

Self was never meant to be the center. We live in a selfish pleasure-centered culture. The prevailing diagnosis of larger society is depression and anxiety, which furnishes all with an excuse to seek more means of escape. The pleasures of sin are only for a small amount of time, and the end of that mirth is heaviness. Many have lived for pleasure only to weep at last that they had wasted all on riotous living. No man has ever devoted their life to the pleasure of their own senses and stated in the end that it was worth it. Even men like Oscar Wilde, who gave themselves to hedonist enjoyments all their life, wept at last on their deathbeds in regret seeking remission. Jacob Marley rightly screamed at Scrooge, "Mankind should have been our business."

4. Henry, Matthew; *Mathew Henry's Commentary on the Whole Bible*.

Suffering is often escaped because we have come to believe that the greatest value and esteem belongs to us and not to those God providentially gave to us. We need a cause greater than self if we are ever to be fulfilled. And that cause comes from faith. "Let nothing be done through strife or vainglory; but in lowliness of mind let each esteem other better than themselves. Look not every man on his own things, but every man also on the things of others. Let this mind be in you, which was also in Christ Jesus. . . ." (Phil. 2:3–5)

Christ is the great example here. It was His mind to esteem others greater than self when He emptied Himself. He could have chosen the way of escape, but He chose to endure the cross for the joy that was set before Him (Heb. 12:1, 2). He did not escape but embraced suffering when He cried "not as I will but as thou wilt." He is the image into which we are to be conformed. "Hereby perceive we the love of God, because he laid down his life for us: and we ought to lay down our lives for the brethren." (I John 3:16) This choice of suffering for the sake of others ultimately brought joy to Christ, and it will ultimately bring joy to us if we embrace it in our pursuit of Him. Centuries of faulty ethical philosophy have convinced our culture that avoiding pain and pursuing pleasure are the ultimate good for the individual and for the collective. True joy, though, comes from suffering for the right reasons and for the greater principles. The psalmist said of those who sow in tears that they will reap in joy (Ps. 126).

Moses further chose to suffer because he esteemed *testimony as being greater than treasures*. The term integrity may well be used instead of the word testimony. It is often integrity that is the first to be jettisoned in the name of escaping suffering. The wife of Job complained that Job maintained integrity and told him to curse God and die. To live for that which is true and that which is good is always greater than to do contrary. Our text stated that Moses was "Esteeming the reproach of Christ greater riches than the treasures in Egypt: for he had respect unto the recompense of the reward."

When the painful event occurs and the fork in the road is seen, will we decide to honor Christ (which is the decision to suffer), or will we choose the way of escape. Moses could have chosen to maintain the status quo. To keep the world and its riches. He was the son of Pharaoh's daughter. The treasures here represent the ease and comforts of the world. It should be noted that the value that Moses saw in Israel was the value of the promises to Abraham of a Savior and a Redeemer which was to come. Moses considered the reproach itself to be riches, greater riches. The truth or promises of Christ were of greater value. Do we value the person of Christ, or do we value our own ease and comfort? Is there a higher truth for us to hold that does not have a for-sale sign on it if the right price was offered?

Christ said of the seed that fell on the stony ground that these were they who embraced the Gospel as long as it was easy, but when affliction and persecution arose for the sake of the Gospel they were offended (Matt 13:20, 21). They chose to escape because they saw Christ to have no value over their own ease. The disciples though, saw the value of Christ, and therefore decided to honor Him through suffering. "And they departed from the presence of the council, rejoicing that they were counted worthy to suffer shame for his name." (Acts 5:41) Thus will each Christian do, those who see the reward and pleasure of Christ more important than the praise of men.

To stand up for Christ in this world will require us to endure hardness for Him; to leave our comfort for Him. To take up the cross of a testimony for Christ He will need to be esteemed as the greatest treasure, altogether lovely. Christ lived and endured the contradiction of sinners against Himself for us. He bled and died for our sin that we might have heaven. Shall we choose escape? Demas forsook the work because he loved the present world. Many stopped following Christ when His words became too hard. Moreover, Christ is asking us, "Will you go too?" There is recompense. There is a crown to be won. There is something far greater than our own present ease.

Moses finally chose suffering because he saw *the sight of God as being greater than the strength of the king*. "By faith he forsook Egypt, not fearing the wrath of the king: for he endured, as seeing him who is invisible." Moses suffered and endured because He saw something greater than the temporal earthly rule. He was not afraid of Pharaoh and his armies. He was not afraid of men. He saw the one that was over all things. When the painful event comes, we are left with a decision. Will we choose the fear of men which is the way of escape, or will we look to God which is not seen and choose suffering? God is the Lord of glory, the Lord of all.

The world and its authority are intimidating. The earthly kings have always told the Christian not to preach the Gospel. But the apostles of old told us that we ought to obey God rather than man (Acts 5:29). This is the way of suffering, and it is only possible by walking by faith and not by sight. I have never seen God with my naked eye, but I know He is there, and He is higher than all. He is the true authority, and I must obey Him. There is a deeper and more intrinsically valuable presence in all that we do. We need to seek that greater reality. If one chooses to escape in this context, it is because they see nothing greater than the authority of men. We escape by our compliance to worldly authority and societal pressures because it is deemed by us to be too hard to swim against the tide. Nevertheless, when we see God the way He is, we can take up any cross.

What will you do with your pain? The question itself is a question of value. Do we value ourselves and our own needs or do we value the needs or others (specifically the people of God), the testimony of Christ, and the reality and authority of God more? If so, there arises meaning and value to all manner of suffering that we may encounter in this life. As such, we cannot only draw comfort in them, but also our suffering becomes a conduit of comfort to others through them. If we value ourselves only, we will always seek to escape the cross. Nevertheless, if we value the higher principles more, then we will choose rather to suffer. We have been called to suffer and to endure hardness. If we suffer with Christ, we shall also reign with Christ. Suffering purifies and makes us of value to others and ourselves. And above all it provides the context in which we may honor our Lord.

www.ingramcontent.com/pod-product-compliance
Lightning Source LLC
Chambersburg PA
CBHW060402090426
42734CB00011B/2238